OREGON TRAIL® II

The Official Strategy Guide

Now Available
Computer Game Books

The 7th Guest: The Official Strategy Guide
Alone in the Dark 3: The Official Strategy Guide
Betrayal at Krondor: The Official Strategy Guide
Buried in Time: The Official Strategy Guide
CD-ROM Games Secrets, Volume 1
Celtic Tales: Balor of the Evil Eye–The Official Strategy Guide
Cyberia: The Official Strategy Guide
Descent: The Official Strategy Guide
DOOM II: The Official Strategy Guide
Heretic: The Official Strategy Guide
Kingdom: The Far Reaches–The Official Strategy Guide
King's Quest VII: The Unauthorized Strategy Guide
The Legend of Kyrandia: The Official Strategy Guide
Lode Runner: The Legend Returns–The Official Strategy Guide
Machiavelli the Prince: Official Secrets & Solutions
Marathon: The Official Strategy Guide
Master of Orion: The Official Strategy Guide
Master of Magic: The Official Strategy Guide
MechWarrior 2: The Official Strategy Guide
Microsoft Space Simulator: The Official Strategy Guide
Myst: The Official Strategy Guide, Revised Edition
The Pagemaster Official CD-ROM Strategy Guide and Companion
PowerHouse Official Secrets and Solutions
Prince of Persia: The Official Strategy Guide
Sid Meier's Civilization, or Rome on 640K a Day
Sid Meier's Colonization: The Official Strategy Guide
SimCity 2000: Power, Politics, and Planning
SimTower: The Official Strategy Guide
Spaceword Ho! Official Secrets and Solutions
Terry Pratchett's Discworld: The Official Strategy Guide
TIE Fighter: The Official Strategy Guide
TIE Fighter: Defender of the Empire–Official Secrets & Solutions
Under a Killing Moon: The Official Strategy Guide
WarCraft: Orcs & Humans Official Secrets & Solutions
X-COM Terror From The Deep: The Official Strategy Guide
X-COM UFO Defense: The Official Strategy Guide

How to Order:

For information on quantity discounts contact the publisher: Prima Publishing, P.O. Box 1260BK, Rocklin, CA 95677-1260; (916) 632-4400. On your letterhead include information concerning the intended use of the books and the number of books you wish to purchase. For individual orders, turn to the back of the book for more information.

The Official Strategy Guide

Wayne Studer

PRIMA PUBLISHING

To the memory of Anna Reeves, born on the Oregon Trail in 1866.

PRIMA'S SECRETS OF THE GAMES is a trademark of Prima Publishing, a division of Prima Communications, Inc.

P™ is a trademark of Prima Publishing, a division of Prima Communications, Inc. Prima Publishing™ is a trademark of Prima Communications, Inc.

Important:
Prima Publishing, Inc., has made every effort to determine that the information contained in this book is accurate. However, the publisher makes no warranty, either express or implied, as to the accuracy, effectiveness, or completeness of the material in this book; nor does the publisher assume liability for damages, either incidental or consequential, that may result from using the information in this book. The publisher cannot provide information regarding game play, hints and strategies, or problems with hardware or software. Questions should be directed to the support numbers provided by the game and device manufacturers in their documentation. Some game tricks require precise timing and may require repeated attempts before the desired result is achieved.

ISBN: 0-7615-0367-5
Library of Congress Catalog Card Number: 95-74913
Printed in the United States of America
· 96 97 98 BB 10 9 8 7 6 5 4 3 2 1

CONTENTS

Chapter 13   Trail Maps in Oregon Trail II 153

Chapter 14   Historical Characters in Oregon Trail II 173

PREFACE

More people have used *The Oregon Trail*® in one of its many versions than any other educational software. The original western trail simulation was a mainframe timeshare program before microcomputers even existed. And this classic has since been MECC's best seller, with every new version rising to the top in sales.

In fact, MECC (Minnesota Educational Computing Corporation) has produced more educational software than any other company. MECC has helped supply thousands of schools across the country with a library of software. In short, MECC has been a leader in educational computing since the very dawn of "educational computing" itself.

So it's with tremendous pride and pleasure that we now unveil *Oregon Trail*®*II*. Following the 1993 edition of *The Oregon Trail*, it's been totally re-designed from the bottom up with advanced CD-ROM capabilities.

I've taken part in this project from its very beginning, serving as director, co-designer, historian, and writer, and I'm honored to work for a company that places the educational needs and interests of children first. I work with a terrific, talented group of people, and if you have half as much fun using *Oregon Trail II* as we had making it, you're in for a real treat.

I hope this book helps makes your use of *Oregon Trail II* an enjoyable, rewarding experience. Have fun learning, and happy trails!

Wayne Studer
Summer 1995

THE HISTORY OF THE OREGON TRAIL

The Historical Trail Itself

The 1840s and 1850s were the peak years of westward migration over the Oregon Trail. Every spring, hundreds and often thousands of people would gather at one of the popular jumping-off towns, buy the supplies they would need, and set off. Wagon trains could be a few wagons or as large as a hundred. It was one of the biggest voluntary mass migrations in human history.

The Oregon Trail and later the California and Mormon Trails were blazed during the first half of the nineteenth century by intrepid explorers who themselves were often following American Indian trails. Meriwether Lewis and William Clark were among the earliest and most famous to cover part of the Oregon Trail, but there were others. Men such as Robert Stuart, Thomas Fitzpatrick,

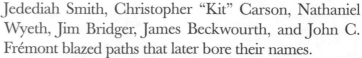

Jedediah Smith, Christopher "Kit" Carson, Nathaniel Wyeth, Jim Bridger, James Beckwourth, and John C. Frémont blazed paths that later bore their names.

By the late 1830s, Americans living in the East began to view the territory west of the Mississippi River with increased interest. As reports filtered back of the far-western country, more and more adventurers were determined to settle the new land.

They also hoped to claim it for the United States. The Oregon Country (which included all of the present states of Oregon, Washington, and Idaho, plus parts of Wyoming, Montana, and British Columbia) was jointly controlled by Great Britain and the U.S. Both countries had strong claims to the region. The equally attractive territory of California, plus other lands due east, were part of Mexico. No matter. American settlers were already striking out.

Although some groups headed out earlier, 1843 is often recognized as the start of the Oregon Trail. This was the year of the "Great Migration," when John Gantt and Dr. Marcus Whitman led 875 people out of Independence, Missouri. The following year more than a thousand people traveled west in covered wagons.

At first they headed to Oregon's fertile Willamette Valley, but in 1846 a popular new trail sprang up. Its destination was the Great Salt Lake Valley, reached via the Mormon Trail. This new trail began at Nauvoo, Illinois, when Brigham Young led the first group of Mormon emigrants to the Great Salt Lake.

Before 1849, relatively few pioneers were bound for California, although the California Trail was known and in use. Until the discovery of gold in 1848, Oregon remained a far more popular destination.

Not everyone who went to Oregon had their eyes on the Willamette Valley in the northwestern part of the state. The Rogue River Valley in southwestern Oregon was also popular. And the opening in the late '40s of an offshoot from the California Trail—the Applegate Road, later known as the Lassen Road or the Applegate-Lassen Road—allowed settlers to flood into southern Oregon.

The great era of wagon trains on the western trails was over by 1860. After the Civil War, most of the people who went west would travel by stagecoach, railroad, or ship. Small groups of wagons would continue west over the old trails as late as the 1880s, but in decreasing numbers.

Here are some facts about the western trails that you may find especially interesting:

- From 1840 to 1860, the total number of people who traveled the Oregon, California, and Mormon Trails in wagon trains is estimated to have been between 315,000 and 320,000—well over a quarter of a million people.

- Although most pioneers survived to begin their new lives in the West, death was a frequent visitor. There was roughly one grave for every 200 yards of trail, and many of the victims were elderly people or children.

- The four most common causes of death on the trails were cholera, wagon accidents, drownings during river crossings, and accidental gunshots.

- Contrary to popular belief, very few pioneers were killed in Indian attacks. During the entire period from 1840 to 1860, fewer than 350 died at the hands of Native Americans. In fact, Indian attacks were extremely rare, especially in the early years. It wasn't until the Indians lost their land and buffalo and took sick with new diseases that things changed.

✸ Also contrary to popular perception, most pioneers were not poor people desperate for a second chance. They were folks who could afford to buy all the supplies needed for such an expensive journey. In fact, the cost often amounted to three years' wages for the average person. Thus, most of the people who traveled the western trails led comfortable lives back east, but yearned for even greater opportunity.

✸ Few rode in their wagons, which were usually loaded with valuable supplies. Only very young children, the elderly, and the sick had the luxury of riding.

✸ Wagon trains rarely traveled in single file. Instead, whenever possible, they spread out to avoid choking on each other's dust.

✸ Wagon trains formed a circle overnight or during rest periods, but not for protection. It was to corral their animals, making them less likely to stray. For this reason, emigrants always sought out grassy areas for their campsites.

✸ Although nearly every wagon party hunted, it was not the chief source of food. Before setting out on their journey, travelers were advised to stock up on all the food they would need. Hunting was unreliable, especially by the late 1850s, when buffalo and other game became scarce. In addition, pioneers needed a lot more than just meat to survive.

✸ The most common deficiency disease on the trails was scurvy, caused by a lack of vitamin C. People in the nineteenth century didn't know about vitamin C, but they knew that fruits and vegetables, especially when fresh, could prevent scurvy. But because fresh fruits and vegetables were hard to come by, they would eat pickles, an excellent source of vitamin C. Vinegar is another good source; travelers would create a drink similar to lemonade with watered down vinegar and sugar.

The Educational Simulation

The Oregon Trail began more than 20 years ago, when Don Rawitsch, Paul Dillenburger, and Bill Heineman devised the original program. Then student teachers in the Minneapolis Public Schools, the three used a teletype machine and a mainframe computer to create the original text-based version. It had no sound or graphics, and sixteen students used terminals physically removed from the mainframe to play simultaneously. To hunt, students had to type BANG quickly enough to shoot game. Then they had to wait several seconds before learning whether their hunt was successful. (For those old enough to remember, do you recall those magic words "Good eatin' tonight"?)

When Don Rawitsch joined MECC in 1973, he brought *The Oregon Trail* with him. Employing more powerful mainframe technology here, several hundred students could take part in the simulation at the same time. But the program was still entirely text-based. And so it remained for the next several years. Nevertheless, *The Oregon Trail* continued to grow in popularity.

In 1979, *Oregon* came out on floppy disk for the Apple II. It was one of several programs grouped together called *Elementary Volume 6*. For the first time, students all over the country could enjoy this historical simulation. There were now simple graphics and sound, primitive by today's standards, that were a major breakthrough for the time. *Elementary Volume 6* quickly became MECC's best-selling product, almost certainly because of *Oregon*'s popularity.

This was the dawn of the microcomputing age, and *Oregon* was the first hit program in the educational field. In fact, as *Oregon* grew, so did the use of microcomputers in schools. The two phenomena fed each other. Apple II soon dominated the school computer market, and the whole field of educational software developed, making *Oregon* a founding program in the field.

Later versions of *Oregon*, still part of *Elementary Volume 6*, were developed for Atari, Commodore 64, and Radio Shack computers. But the next really big step took place in 1985, when Apple II Version 1.0 of *The Oregon Trail* first appeared. Now home computers were having a major impact, and *The Oregon Trail*, with its historical accuracy and enhanced graphics and sound, became a bestseller.

Other versions of *The Oregon Trail* followed: Apple IIGS and networkable Apple versions in 1987; an MS-DOS version in 1988; and an enhanced VGA/MCGA version for MS-DOS in 1991. Also in 1991, MECC introduced *Wagon Train 1848*, a Macintosh-only, co-operative-learning version of *The Oregon Trail*. Here students playing together over a network could link up their computers to form wagon trains, each Mac being a separate wagon in the train. The Macintosh version of *The Oregon Trail*, with a whole new desktop interface and vastly improved graphics and sound, followed soon after. And in 1992, the program's desktop interface moved over to MS-DOS, sporting high-resolution VGA graphics, digitized sound, MIDI music, and other enhanced features.

Then the first CD-ROM versions of *The Oregon Trail* (MECC's first CD-ROM product) appeared in 1993 and quickly became bestsellers. But even as these first CD-ROMs were being shipped, MECC was making plans for an all-new version. *Oregon Trail II*, the culmination of nearly two full years of research and development, is the first of a new generation of programs. It's so different, so much more advanced, that its name demands those Roman numerals.

In short, the trail will never be the same again.

How Is Oregon Trail II Different from the CD-ROM Version of The Oregon Trail?

As much as it pains us to disparage such a fine old friend—an indisputable classic in its field—*The Oregon Trail* just can't match *Oregon Trail II*. Here's a head-to-head comparison of the two:

THE OREGON TRAIL CD-ROM	OREGON TRAIL II
The Oregon Trail and three cutoffs	The Oregon, California, and Mormon Trails plus more than a dozen cutoffs
No choice of year of travel—just 1848	A choice of 21 years of travel, 1840–1860, with the trail and its landmarks actually changing from year to year
One jumping-off town: Independence, Missouri	A choice of four jumping-off towns: Independence, Missouri; St. Joseph, Missouri; Nauvoo, Illinois; and Kanesville/Council Bluffs, Iowa

continued

THE OREGON TRAIL CD-ROM	OREGON TRAIL II
Only one destination: Oregon City	A choice of four destinations: Willamette Valley/Oregon City (northern Oregon); Rogue River Valley/Jacksonville (southern Oregon); Sacramento, California; and Salt Lake City, Utah
Fewer than 20 landmarks on the trail	Nearly 250 landmarks on the trail
A choice of eight different occupations	A choice of 24 different occupations plus the option to choose additional skills
One level of play	Three levels of play allowing you to choose between an ordinary member of the wagon train, the elected captain, or a hired trail guide
Fewer than 20 characters	Nearly 200 characters, many with names and colorful personalities (most of whom have different things to say at different times and places), with more than 1,000 conversations and over three hours of digitized speech
Challenges: river crossings, rafting down the Columbia, and a relatively small set of events	In addition to river crossings and rafting down the Columbia, there are hills to climb and descend, deserts to cross, and a greatly expanded set of events

continued

THE OREGON TRAIL CD-ROM	OREGON TRAIL II
Graphics: all images hand-drawn	Images produced by a variety of state-of-the-art techniques, including digitized and digitally manipulated photographs and video, as well as 3-D renderings
No special graphics for towns and forts	3-D rendered towns and forts with multiple scenes, enabling you to explore the site and enter buildings
Sound: 30 digitized sounds	Over 100 digitized sounds
Music: a small set of popular tunes from the period in simple arrangements	A completely orchestrated original soundtrack plus newly arranged popular tunes of the period and authentic Native American music
An on-line guidebook with a few dozen definitions and descriptions	An on-line glossary with hundreds of entries and a detailed guidebook, based on actual publications of the time, which changes from year to year
An on-line exportable trail log that keeps track of daily events	An on-line exportable diary that not only tracks daily events but allows you to enter text of your own

Let's put it this way: Whatever *The Oregon Trail* does, *Oregon Trail II* does bigger and better.

MODELS FOR OREGON TRAIL II

The Real Journey

Oregon Trail II takes you on the journey of a lifetime, where you'll experience the adventures of the pioneers who went west in covered wagons from 1840 to 1860. Adventures are based on actual diary accounts, documents, and research (as noted in the bibliography).

Diaries of the period are filled with harrowing accounts of the pioneers who faced accidents, illness, and injuries. They struggled at river crossings and steep hills. They lost animals and wagon parts, and ran out of food and water. They were at the mercy of the weather—snow, wind, rain, or blazing sun. And to top it off, treks were long and full of life-and-death decisions.

Just as in real life, events and decisions in *Oregon Trail II* will affect your journey and the health of your party. For example, you decide what to do when heavy rains swell the rivers and make them dangerous to cross. You must weigh the consequences when you over-pace the draft animals, skip rest, or eat poorly, all of which will increase your likelihood of accidents and illness.

But you'll also have the fun of visiting forts, trading posts, and towns that existed then, where you can stop to rest or explore, have conversations, and—if you have the money—buy supplies. Most of the well-known landmarks of the western trails appear in *Oregon Trail II*. Some are abandoned or grow through the years, and some change their names. All are historically accurate.

Underlying Models

Because *Oregon Trail II* is based on real life events, you'll experience the same weather, health, and trail conditions as the pioneers, with only your personal skills to guide you.

Weather provides a good example of how the *Oregon Trail II* models work. Most of the weather in the simulation is generated randomly based on both the average and extreme temperature and precipitation patterns for many sites along the western trails. Daily temperature and precipitation affect health, river depths, the condition of the trail, the availability of water and grazing, and more. Even the melting of snow and the evaporation of surface water is taken into account.

Some cases of historically significant weather-related events are "forced" by the weather model to occur, such as the notorious "Donner Party Blizzard" of late October 1846. In other words, since heavy snow in the Sierra Nevadas is possible in October during any year, and because the aforementioned famous blizzard happened in the Sierra Nevadas in October, *Oregon Trail II* will always generate heavy snow in the Sierra Nevadas in October 1846. In addition, dangers ranging from cholera to broken wagon parts, from locusts to severe thunderstorms, are also generated by real patterns.

For instance, your chances of suffering a broken wagon axle are affected by the weight of your load, how long your wagon has been on the trail, and the condition of the trail itself. You'll also have to worry about your current pace (a broken axle is more likely if you're traveling over eight hours per day), and whether you have grease for lubricating axles and wheels and turpentine for treating wagon parts against the weather. Have you recently visited a blacksmith shop at a town or fort? Should you try to fix the part, replace it with something from your supplies, or trade for a replacement? It all depends on your skills, whether or not you're a blacksmith or carpenter, and if you carry tools and spare parts.

And that's just wagon axles! While other models are too many and too complex to describe here, just keep in mind the necessity of resting from time to time. Resting has a major influence on your health. Regular rests of a day or two help keep both you and your animals fit. And resting is *almost* always one of the best responses to illness or injury.

Remember probability, too. There are few guarantees in *Oregon Trail II*. For example, if you're a doctor in the simulation, or have medical skills, it increases your party's chances when hurt or sick, but doesn't guarantee recovery. And it doesn't override the importance of making good decisions. A doctor who makes a bad decision won't fare better than a person without medical skills who makes a good decision. The doctor will probably fare worse. But a doctor who makes a good health decision has a greater chance than a person without medical skills who makes the same decision. *Usually*.

The Guidebook

The on-line guidebook feature of *Oregon Trail II* provides a large number of hints that should help you deal with the challenges posed by the simulation. For in-

A Practical Guide to the
OVERLAND TRAILS
in the Western Regions
of
NORTH AMERICA
including
a Detailed Itinerary
and
Sound Advice
for the
Judicious Emigrant

1840 Edition

stance, it discusses various strategies for crossing rivers, the best treatments for illnesses, and more. Although the guidebook feature is not as extensive as this strategy guide, it is a very useful supplement.

HINTS FOR ACHIEVING HIGHER SCORES

It's difficult to say what the highest possible score is in *Oregon Trail II*, since so many factors are taken into account, but it can be 25,000 points or more. By contrast, the lowest possible score is probably 625. Scoring is achieved only with successful completion of a journey. Making it to your final destination point and facing many other elements determine your score. Below are some suggestions to help you earn the highest possible scores.

Your Level of Play

At the start of a journey, on the Character Creation screen, you can choose to be a Greenhorn, Adventurer, or Trail Guide. Since Greenhorns don't make decisions at trail splits and aren't responsible for the wagon train, they don't receive bonus points for the wagon train's success. On the other hand, Adventurers and Trail

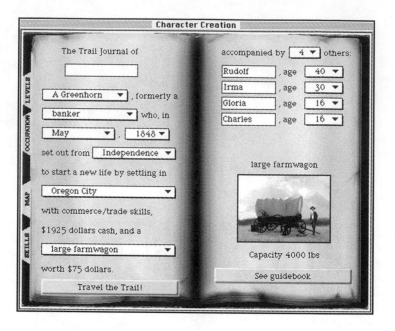

Guides do have these added responsibilities, and do receive wagon train bonus points.

As an Adventurer or Trail Guide, you gain wagon train bonus points in several ways. Most importantly, you must guide your wagon train to its chosen destination. You get points for the number of wagons and people who survive the journey and for their overall health and morale. Points are deducted for every person who dies along the way and every wagon that doesn't make it.

In addition, Trail Guides get paid for their work: $500 at the start of the journey and $1,000 at its end—that is, *if* they reach the destination chosen at the start of the game. Since final cash is calculated into the scoring, this extra money translates into additional points.

This means Adventurers and Trail Guides usually achieve higher final scores than Greenhorns. Keep in mind, however, Greenhorns don't have to worry about wagon train morale. If morale falls too low, Adventurers are voted out of office and are demoted to

Greenhorns. Unless you're lucky enough to be voted back in if morale doesn't improve under the new leadership, you remain a Greenhorn and have lost your bonus points. As for Trail Guides, they're *fired* if morale falls too low, and the game automatically ends with no score at all.

The Length of Your Journey

Your final score is affected by how long your journey takes. For every combination of starting and ending points in *Oregon Trail II* (such as Independence to Oregon City, or St. Joseph to Sacramento), there's an optimum mileage figure. This figure is the shortest number of miles needed to reach your destination. The shorter your journey, the fewer points you get on completion. Of course, longer journeys are more challenging and easier to fail, so choosing one may not be the best strategy until you've gained more experience.

The following chart shows the number of points you'll receive for successfully traveling the various routes in *Oregon Trail II*. Note that the longest journey of all is from Nauvoo to the Willamette Valley/Oregon City, a trip of nearly 2,500 miles.

FROM \ TO	Willamette Valley/ Oregon City	Sacramento	Rogue River Valley/ Jacksonville	Great Salt Lake City
Independence	814 points	738	767	427
St. Joseph	804	728	757	417
Kanesville/ Council Bluffs	720	644	673	333
Nauvoo	817	743	772	432

Watch out for the duration penalty at the end of the game. If you take more time to travel a trail than the pioneers usually did, you'll lose a point for every day over the historical figure that you use. The shortest trip, from Kanesville/Council Bluffs to Great Salt Lake City, generally took less than three months. By contrast, the longest journey, from Nauvoo to the Willamette Valley/Oregon City, usually took nearly six months.

The following chart shows the number of days you have to complete each journey before the duration penalty sets in. Notice that *Oregon Trail II* is liberal in its time allotment; for instance, although the journey from Kanesville/Council Bluffs to Great Salt Lake City was usually completed in about 92 days, you get a full 118.

FROM	TO Willamette Valley/ Oregon City	Sacramento	Rogue River Valley/ Jacksonville	Great Salt Lake City
Independence	202 days	188	194	135
St. Joseph	200	186	192	133
Kanesville/ Council Bluffs	185	171	177	118
Nauvoo	203	189	195	136

Now, this doesn't mean you should *rush* your journey, avoiding stops for rest. Pioneers regularly halted along the trail, and those rests are taken into account in the time figures. If you don't take regular rests, your health will suffer. You'll probably have more accidents too, causing greater delays. Better to lose a few points from a possible duration penalty than to lose *far* more because of ill health and the deaths of people and animals. In short, *remember to rest!*

Your Chosen Year of Travel

In *Oregon Trail II*, you can choose to travel in any year from 1840 to 1860, a span of 21 years. The western trails changed significantly during this period. Shortcuts and alternate routes opened up. New towns, forts, and trading posts appeared along the way. Free bridges, toll bridges, and ferries were established at river crossings. And relations with Indians changed.

Though the trail may be easier in some ways in the early years (there were fewer shortcuts and alternate routes, making wrong turns or going in circles less likely), there were far more disadvantages, the worst being the lack of towns, forts, trading posts, bridges, and ferries. Therefore, you get more points for traveling in the early years. Just watch out: If you're inexperienced, it's hard to survive in the wilderness.

Your Chosen Month of Departure

You can choose any month from February to August to start your journey. It makes no difference on your initial points. But choose wisely. February and probably March are too early, since in winter and early spring cold weather and snow are likely. There will also be a shortage of grass for your draft animals. By contrast, June is too late. You probably won't reach your destination before winter. Your best bet is to leave in April or May.

Your Success in Reaching Your Chosen Destination

If you're playing at the Greenhorn level, you *will* reach your destination if you don't die along the way. The computer, functioning in the role of wagon train captain, will lead you there, always choosing the best route at splits in the trail. That's why Greenhorns don't receive bonus points for reaching their destination.

On the other hand, Adventurers and Trail Guides must successfully lead a wagon train. If, as an Adventurer or Trail Guide, you make it to your destination, you receive 1,000 bonus points. In addition, Trail Guides earn full pay as hired guides, thus adding still more to their score. But if you don't reach your chosen destination, you receive only 200 points. (You did, after all, lead them *somewhere* nice). And Trail Guides also forfeit their final pay. So it's definitely in your best interest to *remember* where you chose to go and *get* there.

The Size and Health of Your Wagon Party

At the start of your journey, you either create a wagon party of your own or accept the one the computer creates for you. A wagon party (not to be confused with the entire wagon *train*) must consist of at least three people and no more than six, yourself included. At the end of your journey, you earn bonus points for those who've survived. The better their health, the higher your score. To maximize your score, pick a large party.

Animals, Cash, and Supplies

You also earn points for the number of animals, the amount of cash, and the stock of supplies you still have at the end of your journey.

You have three choices of draft animals to pull your wagon: horses, mules, and oxen. Each animal provides you with exactly the same number of points at the end, so your choice makes no difference in that respect. On the other hand, this choice is very important because your draft animals can help you survive. There are advantages and disadvantages to each type.

Horses are the most expensive, and though they're faster than mules or oxen, they're also weaker. They're more prone to theft or straying, too, and need oats (an extra expense) on the trail.

Oxen are the slowest but also the strongest and cheapest. They're less likely to stray or be stolen than horses or mules, and can get along perfectly well on the grass and other vegetation they find on the trail. Historically, oxen were the draft animals of choice for the pioneers. In fact, given all the supplies you have to take, *oxen are probably your best bet* in *Oregon Trail II*.

Mules fall between horses and oxen in their cost, speed, strength, and proneness to straying or theft. They can be stubborn at times, but they do the best in extreme heat. (Oxen, by contrast, do best in extreme cold.) And though, unlike horses, they don't *require* oats, they do better with them than without.

Your Unused Skill Points

You start each game with 120 skill points that can be spent on various skills that help you during your journey. Certain skills come automatically with certain occupations. For instance, a blacksmith knows how to repair broken wagons and wagon parts, so if you're a blacksmith the cost of your skill isn't deducted from your points. But bankers *don't* automatically have repair skills, so if you want to be a banker with repair skills, you have to buy them by spending 50 skill points.

Because the various skills you can buy help your chances of success, any skill points you decide not to use are added to your score at the end of the game.

Your Occupation

No other single factor has as great an impact on your final score—and your chances of success on the journey—as your chosen occupation. Different occupations provide different skills and, more importantly, different amounts of starting cash. The more starting cash you have, the easier it is to buy the supplies you need for your journey and pay various tolls along the way. The poorer you are, the greater your challenge, and therefore the greater your reward at journey's end.

In *Oregon Trail II*, nobody has more starting money than a banker, so bankers receive the smallest occupation bonus at the end. By contrast, nobody receives less starting money than a teacher, so teachers receive the largest occupation bonus at the end.

The occupation bonus *multiplies* your base score. For example, if you're a doctor and your base score is 10,000 points, your final occupation bonus is multiplied by 1.2, and your final score is 12,000 points. But if you're a teacher with a base score of 10,000 points, you earn a final occupation bonus multiplied by 5.0, giving you 50,000. Quite a difference!

Of course, poverty-stricken teachers have a much harder time of it than well-to-do bankers, but if you play at the Trail Guide level, teachers and others with poor occupations can *more than double* their starting cash with the Trail Guide pay. This won't affect your final occupation bonus either, so it enhances your chances of success.

Your Wagon

You have a choice of three different types of wagons for carrying your supplies on your journey: a small farm wagon, a large farm wagon, or a Conestoga.

Both small and large farm wagons were popularly known as "prairie schooners" during the later years covered in *Oregon Trail II*. A small farm wagon costs about $60. It's ten feet long and four feet wide and weighs 800 pounds. It can safely hold 3,000 pounds of supplies.

A large farm wagon costs about $75. It's roughly 12 feet long and four feet wide and weighs 1,000 pounds. It can safely hold 4,000 pounds of supplies.

A Conestoga wagon, which costs $100, is the largest of all at 14 feet long, five feet wide, and 1,400 pounds.

It can hold 5,000 pounds of supplies. Few pioneers used Conestogas because their great size and bulk made them ungainly and prone to accidents on the long, rough, and steep western trails. They were more suited to the shorter, more easterly journeys of the decades preceding the years covered by *Oregon Trail II*. Don't get a Conestoga; you'll regret it.

Incidentally, you can have more than one wagon if you wish. You choose your first (and perhaps only) wagon at the very start of the game, during your character creation sequence when you pick your jumping-off point, occupation, and other factors. But if you want an additional wagon, you can buy one at the wagon shop in the jumping-off town. This allows you to carry additional supplies—if you have enough draft animals to pull both of your wagons, that is.

Don't forget the importance of the total weight of your supplies. If your animals aren't strong enough to pull your wagon(s) you won't be able to leave town at all. You'll have to buy more animals or lighten your load, or your animals will quickly start to show signs of exhaustion. An overloaded wagon is also much more likely to have accidents or broken parts.

Other Variables

Some variables in *Oregon Trail II* you have little or no control over. For instance, although you can choose the starting month of your journey and various paths along the way (do you prefer a more northerly or more southerly route?), you have no say over the weather. The weather is controlled by the computer program and can wreak havoc on your journey.

Don't despair. There are many factors you can control. Take a look at the following chapters for strategies to help you complete *Oregon Trail II*.

OCCUPATIONS AND SKILLS

More About Occupations

The different occupations you can adopt at the beginning of each game of *Oregon Trail II* have different advantages. For one thing, some occupations give you more starting money than others, and as a general rule of thumb, the more money you have, the easier your journey will be since you'll have extra cash to buy supplies along the way and to pay bridge and ferry tolls. Again, to compensate for this, the less starting cash you have, the greater your bonus score at the end of a successful game.

In addition to the cash differences, each occupation has special survival kills. If you're a doctor, the members of your wagon party stand a greater chance of recovering from illness and injury. Blacksmiths, carpenters, and wainwrights (wagon-makers) are better at repairing broken wagon parts without relying on their spares. Farmers have animal-related skills; their draft animals are less likely to be to be stolen, to wander off, or to suffer illness or injury. And so on. Keep in mind that none of these skills bring guarantees. If you're a doctor, the people in your party (including yourself) can certainly die, but your *chances* of dying are less. Farmers can still lose animals, but the *odds* are lower.

Below is a list of occupations available in *Oregon Trail II*, beginning with those allotted the highest amount of cash.

banker Bankers start out with $2,000 before buying a wagon. That's generally more than enough for the journey. They automatically have commerce and trade skills, too, which means they tend to get good deals. They don't, however, receive any bonus at the end of a successful game.

doctor Doctors begin the game with $1,900. Since they have medical skills, it increases the likelihood of people in their wagon party recovering from most illnesses and injuries. At the end of a successful game, their bonus multiplies their score by 1.2.

merchant Merchants start out with $1,800. Like bankers, they have commerce and trade skills. Their final score for a successful game is multiplied by 1.4.

pharmacist A pharmacist's starting cash is $1,750. They have two sets of skills, a knowledge of medicine and botany. Botany increases their chances of finding fresh fruit and vegetables along the trail. Their final score after a successful game is multiplied by 1.5.

wainwright Wainwright was a word commonly used for a wagon-maker. Wainwrights start out with $1,700 and blacksmithing skills, which means they're less likely to be stalled by broken wagon parts. And when breaks *do* occur, they have a very good chance of repairing them without having to use up their spares. Their final score is multiplied by 1.6.

gunsmith   Gunsmiths begin with $1,600 cash as well as sharpshooting skills. They're better hunters and can bring down large animals with a single good shot. In addition, they're less likely to suffer accidental gunshot wounds. To obtain their final bonus, their score is multiplied by 1.8.

mason   Masons (stone or bricklayers) start out with $1,500, but have no special skills. Their final score is multiplied by 2.0.

blacksmith   Naturally, blacksmiths have blacksmithing skills. They start out with $1,400 and enjoy a final score multiplied by 2.2.

wheelwright   Wheelwrights (wheel-makers) also have blacksmithing skills. Their starting cash is $1,300 and their final score is multiplied by 2.4.

carpenter   Carpenters have (surprise!) carpentry skills, which, like blacksmithing skills, better their chances of repairing broken wagon parts without drawing on spares. They begin the game with $1,250 and their final score is multiplied by 2.5.

saddlemaker   Saddlemakers start out with $1,200 but have no special skills useful on the trail. Their final score is multiplied by 2.6.

brickmaker   Brickmakers begin with $1,150 and have no special skills. Their final score is multiplied by 2.8.

prospector   Prospectors enjoy an unusual advantage: If they reach Sacramento in 1849 or later and decide to search for gold, they'll find more than anyone else. Otherwise they have no starting skills. They begin with $1,100 and their final score is multiplied by 3.0.

trapper   Trappers, like pharmacists, have dual starting skills: tracking and sharpshooting. They're good hunters and can also find new paths around blocked trails or locate missing people and livestock. They begin with $1,050 cash and their final score is multiplied by 3.2.

surveyor   Surveyors start out with $1,000 and no special skills. Their final score is multiplied by 3.4.

shoemaker   Money is starting to get tight. Shoemakers begin with $950 and have sewing skills. That may not sound like much, but it helps ensure their clothes will last longer on the trail. Their final score is multiplied by 3.5.

journalist   Journalists have $900 and no skills. Their final score is multiplied by 3.6.

printer   Printers begin the game with $850 and no skills. Their final score is multiplied by 3.8.

butcher   Butchers have $800 at the start of the game as well as cooking skills. This means a butcher's food will stretch more, and that members of his or her party will be less likely to suffer from food poisoning. They also benefit from a regular boost to wagon train morale. A butcher's score is multiplied by 4.0.

baker   Bakers also have cooking skills, but they're less affluent than butchers, starting out with only $750. Their final score is multiplied by 4.2.

tailor   Now cash is really at a premium and must be spent wisely. Tailors begin with $700 and, like shoemakers, enjoy sewing skills. Their final score is multiplied by 4.4.

farmer Farmers don't have much money—only $650 at the start of the game—but they do have two abilities: botany, and farming and animal skills. Farming and animal skills are especially valuable in keeping your animals alive and healthy. A farmer's end score is multiplied by 4.5.

pastor Pastors are quite poor in cash, starting out with just $600, but they're rich in spirit. They benefit from a weekly boost to wagon train morale—those inspiring Sunday sermons, you know. Their final score is multiplied by 4.6.

artist They're struggling, you know. They begin their journey with $550 and have no special skills of use on the trail. In return they enjoy a final score multiplied by 4.8.

teacher They were underpaid back then, too. Nobody starts out with less money than a teacher, who has just $500 to his or her name. And no special skills, either. To compensate for these tremendous disadvantages, teachers get the largest final bonus of all: Their score is multiplied by 5.0.

NOTE *Here's something to remember, however, if you play Oregon Trail II at the Trail Guide level. You're hired as a Trail Guide just after leaving the jumping-off town and so receive $500 up front for your services. In this way, teachers and other poor folks can instantly recoup the money they spend in the jumping-off town, and maybe more.*

Skills

In addition to the skills you automatically receive with certain occupations, you can buy others using the 120 skill points allotted at the start of each game. There's no way to buy *all* available skills, and you don't have to buy any if you don't want to because unused skill points are applied to your final score at the end of a successful game. Still, owning a skill may mean the difference between finishing your journey or dying on the trail.

Below is a list of skills in order of cost in skill points.

medical skill

Automatic for doctors and pharmacists but otherwise costs 50 skill points. Medical skills help but don't guarantee recovery. Some diseases, such as rabies, are incurable regardless. And good decisions are still important. A person without medical skill who makes a good decision will do better than a person with medical skill who makes a bad decision. But all things equal, medical skill does improve chances of survival.

riverwork

Not automatic for any occupations, costs 50 skill points. Riverwork lets you cross rivers more easily, though again, good decisions are vital. A player without riverwork skill who makes good decisions will do better than a person with riverwork skill who makes bad decisions.

sharpshooting

Automatic for gunsmiths and trappers, otherwise costs 50 skill points. Sharpshooting gives you several advantages. As a good hunter, you're more likely to hit animals and bring them down quickly (buffalo, bear, moose, and elk, for example, often require more than one shot before falling), and you probably won't suffer from an accidental gunshot wound. Needless to say, you still have to aim carefully. A player without sharpshooting skill who takes careful aim will do better than one with sharpshooting skill who's careless.

blacksmithing

Automatic for blacksmiths, wainwrights, and wheelwrights, otherwise costs 40 skill points. If you have blacksmithing skill, your wagon will fare better, and if parts do break, you are much more likely to be able to fix them without drawing on your spare parts (assuming you have them).

carpentry   *Automatic for carpenters, otherwise costs 40 skill points.* Essentially identical to blacksmithing in that you're more likely to be able to repair broken wagon parts without using up your spares. With this in mind, is there any advantage to having *both* skills? Yes, there is! If you have both blacksmithing and carpentry skills, you are almost certain to repair those parts.

farming/ animals skill   *Automatic for farmers, otherwise costs 40 skill points.* If you have this skill, you'll have fewer problems with your animals along the trail. They're less likely to get lost, stolen, caught in quicksand, sick, injured, or die. No guarantees, mind you—it just stacks the odds a little more in your favor. Remember, good decisions remain important, as always.

tracking   *Automatic for trappers, otherwise costs 30 skill points.* With tracking skills you can locate animals for food and find lost people or livestock. You're also adept at finding new routes when trails are blocked or flooded.

botany   *Automatic for pharmacists and farmers, otherwise costs 20 skill points.* This skill improves your odds of finding wild fruit and vegetables in greater abundance. Now this may not sound like much, but a steady diet of fruits and vegetables is important both to your health and to wagon train morale. And since fruits and vegetables can be hard to find on the trail, anything you do to improve your chances might be a good idea.

commerce/ trade skill   *Automatic for bankers and merchants, otherwise costs 20 skill points.* If you have commerce and trade skill, you'll get better deals. This is especially true in the initial offer and the first one or two attempts at haggling. After that, the benefits of the commerce and trade skill diminish.

cooking: *Automatic for butchers and bakers, otherwise costs 20 skill points.* Folks with this skill enjoy several advantages. They make better use of their food supplies, and are less likely to experience food poisoning. They also get a regular boost to wagon train morale.

musical skill *Not automatic for any occupation, costs 10 skill points.* The only benefit is a regular boost to the wagon train's morale. Of course, that regular boost could prove the difference between continuing as leader and being dismissed.

sewing: *Automatic for shoemakers and tailors, otherwise costs 10 skill points.* Sewing extends the life of your clothes, which tend to wear out or disappear in the course of the journey. Keep in mind that warm clothes and spare clothing can be vital to your survival in winter. They're also highly desirable trading commodities.

Spanish *Not automatic for any occupation, costs 10 skill points.* Along the trail you may meet people who speak only Spanish. This is especially true along the California Trail before 1846. Yet they may have some important information for you—if only you could understand what they're saying! If you can speak Spanish, you'll receive an automatic textual English translation. (Of course, if in real life you happen to be fluent in Spanish, you won't need to purchase this skill, will you?)

SUPPLIES

Before setting out on the trail, you must buy supplies. At the very least, you'll need draft animals to pull your wagon and, unless you want to begin starving right away, some food. You always have the option of buying a basic set of supplies (which *doesn't* include draft animals), and this may get you there. On the other

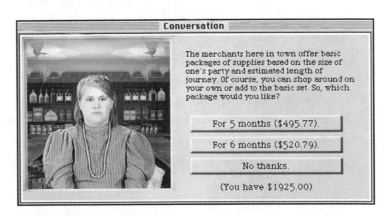

hand, there are supplies that aren't part of your basic set that could greatly increase your chances.

Below is a list of additional supplies, some of which you may want to buy before starting out.

alum　Alum is an astringent used to treat wounds. It is not as good as an antiseptic, and other astringents are available.

anvil　Although an anvil is quite heavy, adding substantially to your wagon weight and thus to the burden on your animals, it might help you repair a broken wagon part without having to use one of your spares.

ax　If you have an ax, you have a better chance of clearing fallen timbers that block your path.

banjo　A banjo adds a small weekly boost to your wagon train's morale.

beads　These are highly desirable trading items with American Indians, if you have enough of them. The Indians in *Oregon Trail II* are pretty sharp traders; they're not much interested in less than $10 worth.

blankets　Blankets have two benefits. They're high in demand among Indians and they decrease your chances of frostbite, freezing, and certain illnesses.

bonnet　Helps keep you warm.

boots　Boots, like blankets and bonnets, help keep you warm. They also help protect against snakebites.

brandy　An antiseptic.

bridle　Bridles help keep your horses and mules from being lost, stolen, or caught in quicksand.

brown muslin cloth Can be used in clothing repairs, so your clothes will last longer.

bullets Although part of the basic set, you should keep an eye on your supply. Without them, your rifle or pistol are useless except as items of trade.

butcher knife If you have one of these, meat is cut more efficiently, thereby lasting longer.

butter churn If you have a milk cow and she's providing fresh milk, a butter churn turns excess milk into butter, which lasts longer before going bad.

camphor Useful as a medicine in some cases.

candles Good for morale.

canteen If you have a canteen, you can go two extra days through dry areas without suffering from thirst.

cash You start out with cash, but don't spend it all at the start. It's always good to have extra for buying supplies and paying tolls.

cast-iron stove Dead weight. This and most other pieces of furniture (kitchen cupboard, grandfather clock, hope chest, rocking chair, and table) serve no purpose except as potential trade items—*if* you can find anyone who wants them, which is unlikely.

chain Useful for going up or down steep hills. In fact, some are so steep that, unless you have a rope or chain, you can't negotiate them, particularly in bad weather. A chain also improves your odds of rescuing an animal caught in quicksand.

checkers board and set   Provides a small weekly boost in morale.

chickens   They lay eggs, a regular source of food, although they won't produce in very dry areas. They're not very hardy; they have a tendency to die early on the trail.

coffee beans; coffee mill; coffeepot   You can't make coffee without them—*all three of them*—and coffee provides a small weekly boost to morale.

compass   Helps you find an alternate path around a trail obstruction. Also, members of your wagon party are less likely to get lost if you have one.

deck of playing cards   Provides a small weekly boost in morale.

Dutch oven   Allows more efficient use of food and reduces chances of food poisoning.

Epsom salts   Good for soaking sprained joints.

fiddle   Provides a weekly boost in morale.

fishing net; fishing pole; fishing spear   If you have any one of these you have a chance of catching fish when you rest near a river or lake—a boost to your food supplies. Without one, you'll never catch fish, although you may be able to trade for some now and then.

flute   Like all musical instruments, provides a regular morale boost.

frying pan   Helps you consume food more efficiently and reduces the odds of food poisoning.

grease   Grease was used to lubricate wagon parts, especially the axles. Without grease, broken wagon parts are likely.

guitar Another morale-booster.

gunpowder Although it's among your basic set of supplies, you can't go hunting without it, so make sure you always have a good stock.

hammer Improves your chances of being able to repair a broken wagon part without using a spare.

harmonica Yes, another boost to morale.

hat Helps keep you warm and healthy.

hunting knife Increases the amount of meat you collect from a hunt.

hydrogen peroxide An antiseptic, good for wounds.

iodine Another antiseptic.

isopropyl alcohol Yet another antiseptic. (Really, just one will do.)

kettle Increases food efficiency and reduces chances of food poisoning.

lantern Good for morale. People are also less likely to get lost if you have one.

lantern oil A lantern's no good without it.

laudanum A very good medicine for intestinal ailments (especially cholera and dysentery), but potentially dangerous.

lecithin A popular remedy for the grippe.

long underwear Helps keep you warm in cold weather.

matches   Very useful both in helping you stay warm and preparing food.

mending yarn   Extends the life of your clothing.

milk cow   Expensive, but she gives milk as long as you're not traveling in dry desert or semi-desert regions. (She needs water to produce milk.) This provides extra food. In a pinch, she'll also help pull your wagon. And if because of near-starvation you decide to kill livestock for food, she's the first to go.

mittens   Very helpful in cold weather.

nails   Increase your odds of being able to repair broken wagon parts without using up your spares.

oats   If you're using horses as your draft animals, they won't last long on the trail without oats as regular horse feed. Mules don't *require* oats, but they do better with them than without. Oxen, by contrast, gain nothing from oats except as feed when no grass is available.

pan   Like all kitchen supplies, helps with efficient food consumption.

peppermint   While not as effective (or as potentially dangerous) as laudanum in helping cure stomach aches, peppermint is better than nothing.

pickax   Helps clear paths blocked by fallen rocks.

pickles   These keep longer than fresh or even dried fruits and vegetables, and prevent scurvy.

pig   Expensive meat on the hoof; they get eaten if you run short of food.

pistol

An alternative firearm, though not as useful in hunting as a rifle or shotgun. Keep in mind that, just like rifles and shotguns, pistols have to be reloaded after every firing. *Oregon Trail II* is set in the days before revolvers.

pitchfork

Helps gather hay for your draft animals, should you choose to do this before setting out across a desert.

pot

Another useful kitchen item.

quinine

The best treatment for malaria.

raincoat

Reduces your chances of catching cold, flu (the grippe), or pneumonia during wet, rainy periods.

rifle

Probably the best firearm to take with you; it's part of the basic set. A rifle is more effective than either a pistol or a shotgun in taking down big game, but it's less effective than a shotgun with small game.

rifle or shotgun sheath

Helps protect your firearm, and reduces your chances of an accidental gunshot wound.

rope

Part of the basic set, useful in getting up and down steep hills and in trying to free animals caught in quicksand.

salt

If you have salt among your supplies, any fish or meat automatically gets salted, which greatly extends its life span.

saw

Helps clear trails blocked by fallen timbers and helps repair wagons without using up spare parts.

sets of clothing

Spare clothes help keep you from falling ill and help you recover if you do. Sets of clothes are the best way of stocking up.

set of cooking utensils   Increases food efficiency and decreases chances of food poisoning.

set of eating utensils   Increases food efficiency, but has no effect on the likelihood of food poisoning.

shot   You can't fire a shotgun without it.

shotgun   The best firearm to use when hunting small game like squirrels, rabbits, and birds. It often doesn't have enough firepower, however, to bring down larger game such as buffalo and bear.

shovel   A shovel improves your odds of clearing fallen rocks. It comes in handy when snowbound. Also makes shorter work of burying people.

skillet   Another useful item for increasing food efficiency and decreasing chances of food poisoning.

soap   Gives a regular small boost to your health and lessens chance of infection following injuries.

socks   Help keep you warm in cold weather.

spare horse or mule harness   Helps keep horses or mules from being lost or stolen.

spare ox yoke; spare wagon parts (axle, tongue, wheel)   These spare parts let you replace a broken item when it can't be repaired. The spare ox yoke is relevant only if you're using oxen to pull your wagon.

spearmint   Like peppermint, this can help counteract an upset stomach.

sulfur   Valuable for treating serious wounds and infections.

tent   Helps you stay warm in cold weather.

tin cup; tin plate	Helps increase food efficiency.
tobacco	A highly desirable commodity in trading, especially with Indians, but only if you have enough of it to be attractive in a trade (at least $10 worth).
turpentine	Used in coating wooden wagon parts, making them more resistant to bad weather. If you have some, the chances of a breakdown are reduced.
umbrella	Like a raincoat, an umbrella helps keep you healthy in wet weather.
vinegar	Good for preventing scurvy; also pretty good for treating colds.
wagon cover	Without one, your food supplies are more likely to spoil because they're exposed to the elements.
washboard	Helps you keep your clothes clean, which extends their life.
water keg	Extremely valuable for crossing deserts or other areas without water. If you have a water keg, you can go as long as six days in arid regions before suffering thirst. Unfortunately, a full keg adds a good deal of weight to your wagon.
whiskey	Believe it or not, a good antiseptic.
winter coat	Helps keep you warm in cold weather. Also a highly sought trading item, particularly among the Indians.
winter scarf	Another item that helps keep out the cold.
witch hazel	An astringent that offers a good treatment for minor wounds.

yeast cake   Increases the food efficiency of flour.

Food

Keep in mind that the preceding list doesn't include wagons and draft animals (discussed earlier), nor does it deal with the obvious benefits of different types of food. Some types of food are included in the basic set of supplies, but others aren't. Food in general, of course, prevents starvation. Meat (bacon, ham, pemmican, salt pork, etc.) helps prevent or cure beriberi. Fruits and vegetables, either dried or fresh, help prevent or cure scurvy. Breadstuffs (biscuits, cornmeal, dried bread, flour, etc.) are cheap yet filling, and they give you the energy you need for life on the trail. Spices (including sugar) make things appetizing, and so help maintain morale.

One more thing: *Don't try to buy a little of everything.* Just because you can buy something doesn't mean you *should.* Even if you have enough money to afford all of this stuff, it could easily overload your wagon, exhausting your animals and causing accidents and broken wagon parts. *Pick and choose wisely.*

OVERCOMING OBSTACLES

Crossing Rivers

Drowning was one of the leading causes of death in the mid-1800s, and in *Oregon Trail II* you have many rivers to cross. Be careful. Even if you don't drown, you can lose your supplies. Always *check the current conditions* before starting out. River levels change with the season and recent weather; water can turn dangerous overnight. Besides, checking the current conditions improves your odds no matter which of the following methods you choose. And finally, consider the weather. Crossing rivers is riskier when it's raining. You may want to wait a day or two, hoping for improvement.

fording

Fording simply means heading into the river and allowing your draft animals to pull your wagon across. Never attempt to ford if the water is over two-and-a-half feet deep. But in a shallow, two feet deep river it's a very quick means of crossing, unless you get stuck in the mud or have an accident, such as a tipped wagon.

caulking and floating

Pioneers would sometimes coat the bottom of their wagons with tar or pitch and then float them across a river, allowing their animals to swim separately. This was called caulking and floating. It's a good way to cross rivers that are more than two feet deep. It does, however, take considerably more time than fording.

taking a ferry

When a ferry is operating, you have a rather safe means of crossing. Not *completely* safe, mind you—accidents are still possible—but definitely safer than fording or floating. Ferries don't run if the water level is too low, though. And you can't take a ferry if you don't have enough money to pay the toll. But you may be able to trade some goods for money if you wish. If you're a Mormon (your destination is Great Salt Lake City), ferries run by Mormons are always free. But not all ferries are run by Mormons.

taking a toll bridge

Bridges provide the best crossing of all. In *Oregon Trail II*, bridges are always completely safe. (If only that were true in real life!) Some bridges are free, in which case you automatically cross over them; you don't even have to stop at the river. But other bridges require a toll. As with a ferry, if you don't have enough money, you can't use the bridge. But you may be able to trade away some goods for the necessary cash.

hiring Indians to help

Some river crossings have Indian guides who'll offer to take you across. You have to trade with them first. They'll generally ask for the equivalent of $10 worth of goods. It may be worth your while to do this. An Indian guide will always choose the best means of crossing (from the options of fording or floating) and this substantially reduces the odds of a stuck wagon or accident.

crossing over ice

If a river is frozen, your choices are severely limited. Fording and floating are out. The ferries won't run and there are never Indians around. (Would *you* be hanging around a frozen river if you had better things to do?) If there's a bridge (either free or toll) you can safely use it. But if there's no bridge, you have two options: crossing over the ice or waiting for it to melt.

Crossing the ice is usually fairly safe if the high temperature for the day isn't above freezing (32°), especially if the temperatures are well *below* freezing or haven't gone above freezing for many days. If the high temperature for the day is above freezing, it may still be possible, but it's *much* riskier. Use caution. Falling through cracked ice is a real danger with serious consequences. If the high temperature is above freezing, it may be best to wait, even if it takes a week or more for the ice to melt.

resting/ waiting

This may be a good idea if it's raining (which makes crossing riskier), or if the river's frozen. It may also just be a good time to rest.

NOTE

If riverwork is among your chosen skills at the beginning of the game, your chances of crossing a river without mishap are improved, no matter which method you choose. (But a good decision by a person without river skills is better than a bad decision by a person with river skills.)

Going Up Hills

Steep inclines—hills, mountains, and canyons—posed another major obstacle to wagon trains. When you come to an uphill climb, be sure to check the conditions of the hill before deciding what to do next. Hills are either not very steep, fairly steep, steep, very steep, or extremely steep, although precise wording may vary.

The following is a list of options for going uphill:

continuing as usual

This should be attempted on not very steep hills only, when the weather is good and the trail isn't muddy or icy. Even then there's some risk. (Of course, there's *always* some risk.)

double-teaming your animals

Double-teaming means that one wagon unhitches its draft animals and doubles them up with the animals of another to pull that wagon up the hill. Then both teams are unhitched, taken back down the hill, and used to pull the second wagon up. This takes twice the time as simply continuing, but your chances are better. Double-teaming helps prevent accidents and is generally the best strategy to use on all but the very steepest inclines, even in bad weather or when the trail is muddy or icy.

lightening your load

If a wagon is overloaded with supplies, it may not make it up the hill, even with a double team. In this case you'll be forced to lighten your load, dumping the supplies of your choice. Sometimes a wagon load might not prevent you from going up the hill, but its excess weight is just enough to cause an accident. So it might be best to lighten your load before even attempting the hill.

using ropes or chains

Here you unhitch your draft animals, lead them up the hill a ways, and then have them pull the wagon up using long ropes or chains. This is a very time-consuming means of going up a hill and is, in fact, rather dangerous. It shouldn't be attempted on hills that aren't particularly steep, when it's considerably riskier than the other methods. On very steep or extremely steep hills, however, it's the method with the greatest chance of success—and sometimes the *only* chance of success, especially when the trail is in bad condition. Keep in mind that using ropes or chains is an option only if you *have* a rope or chain among your supplies. If you need one, you may be able to trade for one. Then again, you may not.

waiting/ resting

Your wagon party might need a rest, or maybe it's raining or the trail is muddy or icy. Waiting a while before climbing up the hill could be a good idea. Then again, it may not do any good at all.

Going Down Hills

Going down hills was much more dangerous for covered wagons than going up hills. Think about it. When going down a hill, you have to worry about *braking* your wagon so that it doesn't run away from you. A runaway wagon can hurt or kill people or animals. Wagon accidents were right up there with drowning as a leading cause of death on the trails, and most happened going downhill. So remember to check conditions first.

continuing as usual

Risky, especially on anything other than a hill that's not very steep.

setting your brake and continuing

This is a much safer strategy on hills that aren't especially steep. Wagons had simple brakes (wood pads that created friction against one or more wheels) that offered some protection against a wagon running away. Still, it may not be enough on steeper inclines, especially if the trail is muddy or icy.

anchoring your wagon

This means attaching a large rock or log to your wagon and allowing it to drag behind, adding friction to reduce the chances of running out of control. Although it takes more time than simply continuing or setting your brake, it's often the safest strategy.

using ropes or chains

A very time-consuming and potentially dangerous method, it's sometimes the best or even the only means possible of descending extremely steep inclines. The animals are unhitched and tied to the wagon with very long ropes or chains, and the wagon is eased down the hill, with the animals themselves acting as brakes. Because of the dangers it poses, this method should only be used as a last resort. Again, remember that you can use ropes or chains only if you *have* them in the first place.

waiting/ resting

As always, waiting a while may offer advantages, especially if the weather or trail conditions are bad.

Crossing Deserts

Although there are a number of semi-desert regions with little or no water on nearly all of the routes in *Oregon Trail II*, there are only three true deserts: The Great Salt Lake Desert (on the Hastings Cutoff), the Forty Mile Desert (on both the Truckee Route and the Carson Route of the California Trail), and the Black Rock Desert (on the Applegate Cutoff). Deserts are fearsome obstacles, much dreaded by wagon trains. Dying of thirst is a distinct possibility.

There are several things you can do ahead of time to improve your chances of getting across. First, buy a canteen or, better yet, a water keg before setting out. Canteens extend by two days the amount of time you can travel without water. Water kegs extend that period by six days, although their weight when full adds a significant burden to your wagon and draft animals.

Canteens and water kegs are always available somewhere in the four jumping-off towns. You may also be able to buy them out on the trail, at forts or trading posts, or even trade for them with fellow travelers. But jumping-off towns are the only place where you can be *sure* to find them. And even if you buy a canteen or water keg at the start of the game, check your supplies periodically, especially after a wagon accident, theft, or fire. You may lose the very supplies you're counting on.

At some point shortly before you get to a desert, you'll usually have an opportunity to gather hay for your animals. These are grassy areas where pioneers generally stopped to put up hay for the ordeal ahead. Since there was no forage in the desert and no drinking water unless it rained, hay helped the animals endure the harsh conditions.

If you're given the option of gathering hay for your animals, you'd be wise to take advantage of it. There's a desert ahead, and that hay can spell the difference between life and death. Incidentally, hay is always available at these key points *unless there's snow on the ground*, in which case you're out of luck. (But, then again, if it's snowing in the desert, you won't die of thirst.)

When you reach the edge of a desert, you'll have the option of waiting until sunset to continue. Wagon trains often waited until almost nightfall to avoid the blazing sun. Then they tried to get across before dawn, rushing as quickly as they could without stopping. Sometimes they succeeded. Often they did not—especially when crossing the Great Salt Desert, which is 70 miles wide and *could not* be crossed in a single night. If they had enough water, they'd usually rest during the heat of the day and then continue again with darkness. But if they were short of water, they kept going, blazing sun or no.

To summarize, here are your best strategies for crossing deserts:

⊛ Buy a canteen or, better yet, a water keg at the jumping-off town. Check on it regularly—especially after accidents, thefts, or fires—to make sure you still have it. If you lose it, try to replace it.

⊛ Gather hay for your animals when given the opportunity.

⊛ When you reach the desert, wait until sunset before continuing.

⊛ Get across the desert as quickly as you can. You can do this by increasing your pace of travel to 12 hours a day. Don't stop or slow down for anything that isn't an absolute emergency. An emergency is a serious risk of death to a human or animal. Remember, you need those animals to pull your wagons.

Once you've reached the next landmark, you've made it across the desert. This would be a good time to take a short rest and return to your normal pace.

EVENTS

In addition to such geographical obstacles as crossing rivers, hills, and deserts, you'll face many other challenges and "events" in *Oregon Trail II* that must be dealt with. Following is a list of these challenges and some of the best strategies to deal with them.

Keep in mind that each situation is different and the outcome largely depends on your circumstances at the time. A wagon stuck in deep sand is no big deal if you and your draft animals are in good health and have plenty of food, but if you're in poor health and are low on food (or worse yet, water), a stuck wagon may spell disaster. Resting, which is often a good response to a health-related problem, may not always be such a good idea—especially if you're low on food, behind schedule, or trying to beat the winter snows.

Carefully consider your overall situation before making any decision on how to proceed.

Negative Events

accidental gunshot

Accidental gunshots were one of the most common causes of death on the western trails, right in there with cholera, drowning, and wagon accidents. In *Oregon Trail II*, the only time you're at risk from an accidental gunshot is during or right after a hunting expedition. If you don't go hunting, you've no risk. But, as you know, hunting may be necessary.

If you count sharpshooting as one of your skills, your risk of an accidental gunshot drops dramatically. Carrying a rifle or shotgun sheath among your supplies also lowers your risk. But if you do suffer a gunshot, clean and dress the wound. Treat it with an antiseptic, if you have one, and rest. As with any injury in *Oregon Trail II*, medical skills give you a better chance for recovery.

alkali sickness

Both people and animals can suffer from alkali sickness, which comes from drinking alkali water. People almost always recover without any special treatment, but animals fare worse—they can quickly die from the ailment. Treatment for both is a dose of vinegar, flour and water, grease, or lard (assuming you have any of these items among your supplies). Resting is a bad idea if you're still in the infected area. Never administer baking soda, which is itself alkali and will only make things worse. If you have medical skills, the people in your party have an even better chance than usual for recovery, but this won't do your animals much good.

animal bite

Animal bites are most likely to occur during or following a hunting expedition. Clean and dress the wound or treat it with an antiseptic. Once in a very great while, an animal bite can lead to rabies, which is invariably fatal.

**animal caught
in quicksand**

This happens in areas known for quicksand or where quicksand forms after a heavy rain. Always try to rescue the animal. That is, unless you're in a desert without a water keg, and you have enough other animals to continue pulling your wagon at the same speed. In this one case, you're better off abandoning the poor beast.

If you do try a rescue, you have a very good chance with a rope or chain. By the same token, if you don't have a rope or chain, odds are you won't succeed—but it's still worth trying.

**animal
injured
stepping in
a hole**

Holes dug by prairie dogs and other burrowing creatures posed a real threat to draft animals along the western trail. Stepping in a hole could lame an animal. Unless you're in a desert, your best bet when this happens is to rest it a day or two. The animal hopefully should recover. Odds are it will. Farming and animal skills help here—this and all other mishaps involving draft animals are less likely to occur if you have them.

**animal killed
by lightning**

A very rare event, but you never know. Watch out during thunderstorms and hailstorms. There's not much you can do about it except continue on your way. You may want to replace the animal right off by trading. Or you can wait until you reach a town or fort and buy another. Incidentally, an animal killed by lightning does have the fringe benefit of adding some meat to your supplies.

**animal
mauling**

If you go hunting in an area where there are bears or cougars, you have a chance of being mauled. Your chances increase if you injure an animal without killing it. (Sometimes it takes more than one shot to bring down a large animal.) Cleaning and dressing the wounds or treating them with an antiseptic is best. Then rest.

animals exhausted   If you've gone a long time without resting, or your animals are trying to pull more weight than is good for them, or if you're traveling over a stretch of rough trail, you can exhaust your animals. Rest at least a day or two so they'll regain some strength.

bad cold   A bad cold may not seem like much of a problem, but remember you're out on the trail. You're exposed to the elements and don't have modern, "over-the-counter remedies." Unless cared for, a bad cold can turn into pneumonia.

Colds are more likely in cold or damp weather, so you're in trouble if you're out of matches for that campfire or you're short of warm clothes. You should rest, get plenty of liquids, or take vinegar (a terrific source of vitamin C).

bad mosquitoes   Mosquitoes were a common annoyance on the western trails, especially along the Platte River. Diaries are full of complaints about them. For the most part, they don't pose any serious threat, although wagon train morale suffers when they're thick. Occasionally someone comes down with malaria, but the symptoms won't appear until long after the infection occurs.

beriberi   Beriberi is a vitamin deficiency caused by a lack of meat and/or fresh green, leafy vegetables. You have to go a pretty long time without this type of food to get it, and children are more susceptible than adults.

If someone has beriberi, they need meat. Buy, trade, or hunt for it. Forget the vegetables; they're too hard to come by out on the trail. Besides, they won't cure the problem as quickly as meat. Medical skills won't help either. But as soon as meat is back in your diet, beriberi will improve.

blizzard

Blizzards were scary on the western trails; getting caught in one was often a death sentence. So travelers tried hard to reach their destination, or at least to cross the mountains (where snow was both more likely and more hazardous), before the storms of winter.

Sometimes, however, blizzards struck early, as with the late October storm in the Sierra Nevadas that trapped the Donner Party. If a blizzard strikes, you may want to wait for better conditions before continuing. But if your food is low, you'd best move on.

Always be sure to have boots and other warm clothing with you; you're much more likely to survive winter storms.

broken bones

Broken bones can happen any time in the normal day-to-day activities of trail life but are more likely during wagon accidents and other mishaps. The best thing to do is set the break and apply a splint. Rest may help.

broken ox yokes, broken wagon parts (axles, tongues, and wheels)

You'll never have a broken ox yoke if oxen aren't among your chosen draft animals, but the other breaks can occur at any time. Watch for them when traveling rough trails and late in your journey, when time, use, and the elements have caused wear.

To help prevent breaks, keep grease or turpentine handy. Better yet, have blacksmithing and/or carpentry skills, or at least visit a blacksmith along the trail. (All you have to do is step into a blacksmith shop, even if you come right back out.)

Despite your best efforts, though, breaks will occur. If this happens, try to repair them. You always have some chance of doing so (that is, of fixing it without drawing on a spare part), especially if you have blacksmithing and/or carpentry skills. You're in luck if you brought an anvil (awfully heavy!) or a hammer and nails.

But what if the break is so bad that even skilled people with the right supplies can't fix it? Use your spares, assuming you have some. It's always a good idea to have a spare of each of these items among your supplies. (But you probably shouldn't carry more than one spare of each item at a time since they'll add to your wagon weight.) If you don't have the right part, find one somehow. Trading is the most likely method since you probably won't be lucky enough to be sitting right at a town, fort, or trading post when a break occurs.

buffalo stampede

If you're traveling through relatively flat country where buffalo roam, watch out for a stampede. Don't try to go on until it passes; you could have an accident or someone could get hurt. You might want to go hunting now, especially if you're low on food.

There'll be buffalo aplenty to shoot, even if it is a waste of bullets since you can bring only a fraction of your kill back to the wagon. But be forewarned: You can get hurt hunting in a stampede.

burns

Burns are a routine injury along the trail, what with campfire tending and cooking. Prairie fires or wagon fires are another threat. Burn sufferers should clean and bandage the wounds or apply antiseptic, never grease or lard.

cholera   The disease known as cholera was the single greatest killer along the western trails in the mid-1800s. In fact, it was one of the greatest killers period, even among those who stayed home. It could kill with shocking speed (sometimes in less than a day) and spread wildly. U.S. President Zachary Taylor died of cholera in 1850.

Despite its deadly nature, there are several things you can do to protect yourself. Don't set out on the trail any later than April. Unsanitary conditions left by others ahead of you increase the likelihood of cholera. By leaving no later than April, you reduce the number of people traveling before you. Don't travel in 1849, 1850, or 1852, which were years of major cholera epidemics. Your odds of contracting cholera are much greater in those years than in any others. Don't travel in wagon trains consisting of more than 100 people because large trains are more likely to experience outbreaks.

If someone does get cholera, give them laudanum (an opium tincture useful in combating the disease) and immediate rest. If you don't have any laudanum, increase fluid and salt to help prevent dehydration, and let them rest anyway. Never give Epsom salts. Increasing rations isn't a good idea, either. If you have medical skills, chances of survival are a little better.

Note, however, that someone in your wagon party may suddenly die of cholera with little or no warning, without your having a chance to do anything about it. That's just the way it is.

concussion   Like broken bones, a concussion can happen any time, especially during a wagon accident. Although a concussion rarely has serious aftereffects, it's probably a good idea to rest for a day or two.

consumption   Consumption is the term commonly used back in the nineteenth century to refer to the disease tuberculosis.

A rare problem, it's most likely to hit those with a chronic condition, and is made worse by cold, damp weather. It's contagious, particularly during its early stages, so when someone suffers an attack, make them rest and stay warm and dry.

cuts and abrasions

These are minor injuries that happen during wagon accidents or other mishaps on the trail. Although they pose little threat, you should definitely clean and dress the wounds or treat them with an antiseptic. If not, they may get infected, which could lead to lockjaw or gangrene.

death of a person

Death is an unfortunate reality on the western trails, especially when you plan poorly. Between four and six percent of those who set out on the trail never made it to their destination—and no doubt the percentage was higher among those who didn't plan carefully or who made poor decisions along the way. If someone in your party dies, whatever the cause, be sure to give them a proper burial. Yes, it takes up to a half-day's travel time, but it's the only morally correct thing to do. Besides, a death is a serious blow to wagon train morale and has even worse consequences if not followed by a proper burial.

In fact, the lack of a proper burial causes an automatic 33% reduction in the overall morale of your wagon train—which may be just enough to get you fired.

death of an animal

Of course, animals can die along the way, too. If a draft animal dies, it's classified as an event. But the loss of a chicken or pig passes without special mention.

There's not much you can do when an animal dies. But if it died from an accident (as opposed to an illness), you'll usually have the option of butchering the meat. This increases your food supplies.

Finally, try to replace the animal quickly if its death slows you down.

delay at a ferry   A ferry can usually take only one wagon across a river at a time. This causes bottlenecks on the road west, where wagons have to wait several days before continuing. If you're in a hurry and don't want to wait your turn, you can choose to ford or float. Just remember the ferry is safer, and a delay can give your party a chance to rest, so it's not time completely wasted.

delay at a river   Even rivers without ferries can cause traffic jams when wagons jockey for position at the best crossing points. There's not much you can do but wait your turn. Take it easy and enjoy the rest.

diphtheria   Diphtheria is a serious illness that usually strikes young children, although adults can get it too. It's contagious, so one case can lead to another. The thing to do for diphtheria is to rest and drink lots of fluids. Patent medicines won't do any good.

By the way, you and your party may or may not be immune to diphtheria. Everybody starts out with a random chance of having already had each contagious disease in *Oregon Trail II*, thus rendering them immune.

drowning   Drownings and near-drownings are always a risk at river crossings. Remember, it was one of the most common causes of death on the western trails. You can easily drown if you have an accident while crossing a river. Even if you survive, it's best to rest for a day or two to prevent complications.

duststorm   Duststorms threaten when you're crossing a great deal of sand or dry, dusty soil. Unless you're in a desert, it's best to wait or at least slow down. You could have an accident, lose an animal, or worse, lose a person. If you are in a desert, you best forge ahead. A duststorm won't kill you, but thirst might.

dysentery

Dysentery is another common trail ailment that could be minor or deadly depending on the victim's health. Laudanum is an effective (though potentially dangerous) treatment, and you can't go wrong increasing the victim's fluid and salt intake. Resting is also a good option. Never administer magnesia. Increasing rations isn't a good bet, either. And don't leave dysentery untreated. Dysentery can become a chronic condition causing a general and lasting deterioration in the health of the patient.

extreme cold

Extreme cold is when temperatures fall below 10° F. If you have matches for campfires, a tent, and warm winter clothes (such as long underwear, hats, boots, winter coats, etc.), you stand a pretty good chance of surviving without serious consequences. But if you're not prepared, bitter cold can lead to frostbite, freezing, and death. It's also unhealthy for your animals.

There's not much you can do except endure it. You can freeze to death as easily resting as traveling.

extreme heat

Extreme heat is a temperature of 95° or higher. This isn't as life-threatening as extreme cold, but it does have a bad effect on your health and morale and the health of your animals. It's deadly if you're out of or away from water.

Old people and children are in the most danger from the heat. Unless you're in the desert or other dry area, slow down or stop and rest.

fallen rocks

Fallen rocks can block the trail in the mountains and are most likely to occur after thunderstorms and blizzards.

Your first choice is to go over the rocks, but watch out for accidents.

Your second choice is to clear the path, especially if you've brought a pick ax or shovel, even though you might hurt yourself trying.

Third, if you have a compass or tracking skills, you can look for another way through—that is, if you aren't afraid of accidents on an unproved trail. Maybe you should take the final option: Sit and wait in hopes another wagon train will come your way. They might help you clear the rocks. Don't worry, you'll get another chance in seven days to choose a different course of action. In short, your best bet is to plan ahead; buy a pick ax or shovel before setting out on the trail and try not to lose it.

fallen timbers   Like fallen rocks, fallen timbers block your trail in thick forests. You have the same options as with fallen rocks, except that you're better off with an ax, hatchet, or saw. The moral of the story: buy tools.

fire in a wagon   You could lose everything here. Wagon fires can happen any time, but never head into a prairie fire if you want to avoid likely calamity. If you try to put out a fire, you can get burned, but you'll save some supplies. If you opt to stay safe, you'll lose a lot of stuff to the flames.

flooded trail   A flooded trail often follows heavy rains or snow melt. You can try to ford the water, but your wagon might get stuck in mud or tip over, losing some supplies. Riverwork skills can help. It's nice to have tracking skills or a compass, too, so you can try finding another path. Otherwise, wait for the waters to recede. Don't expect help from another wagon train; it won't happen. After a seven-day wait you're allowed to try your options again.

food poisoning: Food poisoning was a real threat in the days before re-frigeration and preservatives, especially out on the trail. It can happen to you at any time, especially when it's hot, but isn't as likely if you have cooking skills and the proper utensils.

Food poisoning goes away on its own after a day or two, but it can be risky for those in poor health, the young, or very old. Resting makes sense, as does in-creasing fluids and salt. Spearmint helps calm the stomach, and laudanum is effective (but potentially dan-gerous). Don't increase rations, and never give Epsom salts. In rare cases, food poisoning can turn into chronic dysentery.

freezing: You can freeze when temperatures fall below 32° F. It's a danger anytime you're snowbound or traveling through snow, so keep handy supplies of matches, blan-kets, spare clothes, winter coats, mittens, boots, hats, scarves, and/or long underwear. If someone's freezing, try to feed them warm food or build a fire.

frostbite Frostbite is a problem with cold temperatures, too. Pre-cipitation or being snowbound makes matters even worse. Should frostbite occur, you should gradually warm the affected area; that by far is your best choice. Never rub the injured area with snow, and if not treated properly, watch out for gangrene.

gangrene Speaking of which, gangrene can set in after accidental gunshots, burns, broken bones, and frostbite, when these aren't treated properly. If someone in your wagon party suffers from gangrene, you have only one course of action: amputation. It may sound harsh, but it's the patient's only chance. Otherwise, gangrene will kill within days.

As usual, medical skills improve the patient's chances. But try to remember, an ounce of prevention is worth a pound of cure.

the grippe   What was called the grippe back in the 1800s is called the flu today. Flu season is during the winter months, and it spreads easily once someone's infected. Chances of an outbreak are further enhanced by a lack of supplies (raincoats, long underwear, winter coats, blankets, boots) meant for combating cold and damp weather.

Treat the grippe by resting and taking plenty of fluids. Lecithin might help, if you're lucky enough to carry it, but quinine won't do a bit of good.

hailstorm   Diaries of the western trails are packed with stories of amazing hailstorms. These pose a threat to your wagon train if they frighten animals into running away. And once in a while an animal may be killed by lightning during a hailstorm.

Don't try to travel through the storm; you might have an accident. Wait it out instead. It won't last long.

heavy fog   Heavy fog can occur anywhere and at any time when the conditions are right. People and animals can get lost in fog, and you should be careful on rough trail when visibility is low. The combination of rough trail and fog can significantly increase your chances of a wagon accident. Slow down or wait for better weather.

infection   Nearly any type of wound, including burns and broken bones, can get infected, especially if it isn't properly treated. If you get an infection, clean and dress the wound and apply sulfur (you did bring sulfur, didn't you?) or antiseptic. Don't let an untreated infection turn into gangrene—you know what that means.

injured livestock   Sometimes a draft animal will go lame for no apparent reason. If this happens, slow down or, better yet, rest.

Abandoning an injured animal has a bad effect on morale.

internal injuries   Don't take internal injuries lightly. The victim could easily die. If someone suffers internal injuries after a wagon accident, remember sleeping helps you heal, so rest and give laudanum to kill the pain (even though laudanum carries its own risk).

Never give magnesia. As usual, if you have medical skills it improves the patient's chances.

lockjaw   Lockjaw, today called tetanus, develops from improperly treated breaks in the skin. It may even happen if you've been careful. There's not a lot you can do about it save let the disease run its course. Hopefully the patient is strong enough to survive.

Since one of the chief symptoms of lockjaw is an uncontrollable tensing of the muscles, give laudanum to help the victim relax. Rest and medical skills improve the odds.

locusts   Locusts are a great annoyance and so cause a slight drop in morale. They frighten the animals, too, increasing chances of wagon accidents or straying. You should slow down or wait them out.

losses while rafting   If you raft down the Columbia River, you stand a good chance of hitting rocks or whirlpools—at least until you're an old hand at it. If you hit a rock or whirlpool, or get caught in dangerous cross-currents, your raft will tip. If your raft tips, someone may drown. If it's you that drows, the game's over.

Even if no one drowns, a tipped wagon means a loss of supplies. These losses are reported to you after you've reached safety, which is too late to do anything about them.

malaria   It's rare but you can get malaria from a mosquito bite. This sometimes happens weeks after a mosquito infestation.

If someone in your party comes down with malaria, give them quinine. Otherwise the patient's condition will grow steadily worse, and even if they seem to recover, they can develop chronic malaria. Flare-ups of chronic malaria wear you down over time. Rest may help.

measles   Measles, which even today can be life-threatening, was far more dangerous in the nineteenth century. Many American Indian villages, with little or no natural immunity, were wiped out by measles. Wagon trains suffered as well.

This highly contagious disease usually hits the children (because most adults have acquired an immunity to it), and is best treated by taking rest and extra fluids. Rubbing the skin rash with aloe is soothing, but does little else. Measles can turn into pneumonia if not treated properly, which is a big danger to the elderly.

Medical skills will help a lot here.

missing livestock   Your draft animals can stray at any time, but it's much more likely after heavy fog, severe thunderstorms, hailstorms, blizzards, or duststorms. They may also mysteriously disappear near towns, forts, or other settlements, or after an encounter with strangers along the trail. Animals are less likely to be missing if you have farming and animal skills.

If you do lose your livestock, organize a search party. It costs one day of travel time, but you have a good chance of finding them, especially if tracking is one of your skills. If you're lazy you can wait for the missing animals to return on their own. Good luck.

missing person   Draft animals aren't the only creatures that can suddenly disappear on you. A member of your wagon party can turn up missing at any time. It's more likely after bad weather, though.

If a person is missing, always organize a search party. Failure to do so results in a big drop in wagon train morale—not to mention permanent loss of the missing. If this happens you could lose your job as leader.

You can wait for missing people to return on their own (adults are more likely to do this than children), but their odds of rejoining your wagon party are much greater if you actively go looking for them.

mountain fever

The mysterious ailment known in the mid-1800s as "mountain fever" is probably what we call Rocky Mountain spotted fever today. You can't prevent it; it's just something you may catch in the mountains in summer. Your best strategy for recovery is to rest your patient for a few days and try to control the fever.

pneumonia

People in your wagon party aren't likely to come down with pneumonia unless you've made some earlier mistakes. Remember to treat colds, the grippe, measles, scarlet fever, smallpox, and typhoid so they don't turn into pneumonia. And keep an eye on your old folks. The elderly are much more likely to contract pneumonia than others.

Pneumonia threatens when the weather is cold and damp, or if you're low on warm clothes. You should rest the patient and keep them warm and dry.

prairie fire

Prairie fires on the plains were usually started by lightning, but sometimes by careless people. The late, dry summer prairie grass burned quickly and fiercely. If you face a prairie fire, it's best to wait a day or two until it burns itself out.

Keep your wagons at a safe distance, though even here there's a chance of them catching fire. If you try blazing through, you'll get burnt.

quicksand ahead

Quicksand comes in two varieties: patches that always exist in certain places and patches of heavy sand that turn into quicksand only after heavy rains. You're lucky because, unlike the pioneers, you're warned in advance about quicksand.

When this happens, you can forge ahead and lose an animal, slow down to try and avoid being trapped, or put your weakest animal up front. The latter is a trick the pioneers often used. The team continues forward at a slightly reduced pace with the relative assurance that if any animal were to fall into quicksand, it would be the most expendable one. It works in precisely this way in *Oregon Trail II*.

One other option is to wait for conditions to improve, which in this case is definitely not your best bet. If it's "permanent" quicksand, conditions will never improve, and you'll have wasted a week waiting for the program to give you a chance to choose an alternate course of action (unless, of course, you do need the rest). And even the chances of "temporary" quicksand drying up within a week's time aren't very good. Your best choice: put the weakest animal up front and forge ahead.

rabies

Rabies is an extremely rare but deadly disease. You get rabies by being bitten or mauled by a wild, rabid animal during a hunting trip. If this happens, there's a very small percentage of likelihood that that animal was rabid, in which case you will contract rabies; there is nothing you can do to prevent it. And if a person contracts rabies, he will die. Rabies remains as incurable today as it was 150 years ago, and back then they didn't even have the regimen of shots that now can help prevent it.

If one of your party gets rabies, then give them laudanum to ease their suffering and make them comfortable. At least this way the death won't be so hard on wagon train morale.

scarlet fever   Scarlet fever is more likely to strike children than adults. Once a person has had it, they're immune. If someone in your wagon train comes down with scarlet fever, give them rest and plenty of fluids. Laudanum eases the pain but with the usual risks.

Without proper treatment, scarlet fever can turn into pneumonia.

scurvy   Scurvy is caused by a lack of vitamin C in the diet. Scurvy is one of the oldest and most widespread nutritional disorders, yet it wasn't until the mid-1700s that the Scottish physician James Lind discovered and proved that it could be prevented by regular consumption of fruits and vegetables. By the time of the westward migrations, Lind's discovery was common knowledge, for though nobody knew about vitamin C itself (which wasn't discovered until the twentieth century), they knew that there must be *something* in those fruits and vegetables. Pioneers made sure to bring along some food that prevented scurvy. Of course, fresh fruits and vegetables didn't keep well over the long journey, so they made do with dried fruits and vegetables, pickles, and vinegar. And they rarely passed up the chance to gather wild fruits and vegetables on the trail. You shouldn't either.

And remember, your basic supplies won't last forever. They might be lost to accidents, theft, or spoilage. And even though you can go many weeks without vitamin C before getting scurvy, people's fear of the disease is bad for wagon train morale. Make sure you have some source of vitamin C on hand, especially for the children.

severe thunderstorm   As stated earlier, emigrants often commented in their diaries about the frequency and severity of the prairie thunderstorms, which sometimes were unlike anything they had ever experienced back east. *Oregon Trail II*

doesn't make an event of every single rain shower or thunderstorm that occurs in the simulation's underlying weather model (although rain is regularly reported in the "status panel"), but when there's a *severe* thunderstorm, you have a decision to make. Do you want to continue as usual, slow down, or wait for conditions to improve?

If you have plenty of time and supplies, waiting for conditions to improve is a safe bet. The bad weather will probably last only a day or two. If, however, you're behind schedule or short of supplies, you may wish to move on at a slower pace.

The bad news is, traveling in a severe thunderstorm can cause accidents, stray animals, and poor health. Watch yourself—you also have a good chance of getting stuck in mud.

NOTE

During the spring of 1844, the plains experienced a lengthy period of unusually heavy, almost constant showers. The entire period from March 22 to June 1, 1844, saw only eight days without rain. If you're traveling the early sections of the trail during this period, you will experience this type of weather. Also, from June 9 to 11, 1849, the region around Ash Hollow and Chimney Rock was battered by extremely severe thunderstorms, sometimes accompanied by hail; that, too, is reflected in the simulation.

sick livestock Your animals can come down with a number of mysterious ailments. It could be anything form a stomach upset caused by eating strange plants to a fatal disease. You're in better shape if you have farming and animal skills, but rest your animals anyway. You can try giving them vinegar, grease, or lard; hopefully it won't make them worse. Remember: You need your animals to get where you're going.

smallpox Few diseases have been more dreaded in human history than smallpox. It was very contagious and often fatal. If smallpox didn't kill you, the pneumonia that often followed might. Those lucky enough to survive were often left with disfiguring scars. There was a vaccine by the mid-1800s, but it was hard to come by and many people feared it. So smallpox remained a serious problem until well into the twentieth century.

There's only a slim chance in *Oregon Trail II* of someone coming down with smallpox. Once it happens, however, it's likely to spread. Give rest and remember that if the patient survives, they'll be immune for life.

snakebite

Snakebites were common along the western trails. Travelers often had to walk through rough areas teaming with rattlesnakes. Look for them especially on the north bank of the Platte River.

Boots help prevent snakebites, so provide at least one pair for each member of your wagon party, and keep an eye on them.

Use the tourniquet/suction method to treat a snakebite, and give immediate rest, although resting without any other treatment first is risky. Never continue as usual, even in a desert, and forget lots of exercise unless you want to kill the patient. (Incidentally, if you're allergic to animal toxins you'll die instantly from a snakebite.)

snowbound

Remember the ill-fated Donner Party of 1846? The pioneers did. No one wanted to get trapped in heavy snow, exposed to the cold while their food ran out. Neither should you.

Getting snowbound can happen anytime you're caught in heavy snowfall, so try to end your journey before late fall or early winter. Heavy snows can fall earlier in the mountains than in the lowlands, and later in the spring as well.

If you're caught in snow, double-team and continue. Don't just continue as usual because this puts a strain on your animals and can cause accidents and injury. If you're making little or no progress (signaled by the messages *slow progress* or *no progress* in the status panel), consider lightening your wagon. Of course, you're better off snowbound with a shovel than without. But only wait for snow melt if you expect warm weather soon, and only if you have winter clothes and enough food to get you through.

sprained joint (ankle, wrist, etc.)

Sprains are not a serious threat. You can soak the area in Epsom salts and keep it immobile. Exercise is bad for the patient's health and wagon train morale.

starvation

Some people can go longer without food than others, children being the hardest hit. Don't continue as usual when you're starving unless you're absolutely sure there's a town, fort, or trading post within a day's journey. And don't rest; you'll starve to death resting as quickly as you will traveling. Try to trade for some food— even a little bit may get you to the next stop where you can buy more (assuming you have enough money).

You can choose to go hunting, although depending on where you are and the time of year, your hunting expedition may not succeed. (For instance, you'll never find game in a desert.) If absolutely necessary, you can kill a draft animal for food, which adds a lot of meat to your supplies (even if it is mule or horse meat). Let's just hope you won't need the animal to keep going.

Of course, your best strategy is to avoid starvation in the first place. Check your supplies often and don't let your stock of food get low.

strangers ahead

Strangers ahead of you on the trail pose an interesting dilemma. Should you continue at a distance (trying to avoid them), approach them, or just wait and see what they'll do? If you avoid them, you might miss a chance for trading, so morale will suffer.

If you approach the strangers, they may move away (maybe they're not too eager to talk; after all, to them, you're the group of strangers). Or they may strike up a conversation. If you wait to see what they'll do, there's an even better chance that they'll go on their way without speaking to you. Consider that conversations give a chance to learn information and do some trading. Or you might meet people who are in such dire need that they'll simply ask for something, not offering anything in return. If so, it's up to you to decide whether you want to be charitable. Just remember the effects on morale.

One word of warning: Not all strangers are upstanding citizens. You may find you've been robbed after an encounter.

theft from your wagon

Since we mentioned it, a theft from your wagon can happen anytime, but is more likely after meeting strangers on the trail or stopping near a town, fort, or other settlement. (When there are more people around, there will probably be more dishonest people as well.) If you're robbed, always go in search of the thief. The only exceptions to this are when you're in a desert or when you're running so short of time that you can't spare the half-day or more it may take to find your missing supplies. If you search for the thief, you have a chance of finding your stolen goods, especially if tracking is one of your skills.

thick dust from other wagons

Dust was a big nuisance on the trail, stirred up by the large number of wagons and animals traveling together. Thick dust is likely in *Oregon Trail II* unless it has recently rained or snowed.

You can probably continue as usual, although this strains both people and animals and can cause poor health. Slowing down is a good idea since it allows other wagons to get far enough ahead to cut down on some of the dust. And if you have plenty of time and supplies, waiting for conditions to improve is a good bet.

Finally, if you're traveling at an easy pace (eight hours per day), you can pick it up to ten or 12 hours per day in hopes of getting ahead of the other wagons. But not for long—your health may suffer.

thirst Deserts are the most obvious places where there's no water, but semi-desert regions can be thirsty places, too. Especially watch out along the Lander and Sublette Cutoffs. Rain or snow in a dry region can save your life, but don't count on it.

People can die of thirst with shocking speed, especially children. Plan ahead. Carry a canteen or, better yet, a water keg. Canteens give you two extra days in dry regions, while water kegs allow around six days. When you come to a desert, always travel at night, waiting until sunset to start across. Move as quickly as possible, upping your pace to ten hours or more per day.

Once you finally reach water, rest for a day or two.

tipped wagon

If your wagon tips on the trail or while crossing a river, there's not much you can do but get it upright, clean up the mess, and count your losses before continuing. Try to avoid tipping your wagon in the first place with the following "tips."

Don't take a Conestoga wagon. The big, unwieldy Conestogas were much more likely to tip in rivers, on hills, and over rough trail. Don't over load your wagon. Slow down or wait it out during heavy fog, severe thunderstorms, duststorms, or other bad weather, especially on rough trail. Avoid traveling at the grueling pace of ten or more hours per day. And finally, carefully choose your method of crossing rivers and going up or down hills. A tipped wagon is usually the result of a poor decision.

a turn for the worse
Often when someone is suffering from an illness or injury you'll receive a message saying they've taken a turn for the worse. You must respond according to what's wrong with them. Resting is usually, though not always, a good idea.

typhoid fever
Typhoid fever is contagious, so if one case appears, it could easily spread through the wagon train. The best responses are to rest and/or to try to control the fever. Otherwise victims may lapse into pneumonia. There's not much else you can do, although normally healthy people stand a good chance of recovery.

typhus
Another contagious disease, likely to spread. As always, medical skills increase chances of recovery. The only good option in this case is to rest for at least two or three days.

unknown ailment
Sometimes people get sick and you don't know the cause. If you have medical skills, your chances of diagnosing the disease are better, but not assured. Consider the symptoms and decide on a good course of action—which usually includes rest.

wagon stuck in deep sand
Deep stretches of sand were common dangers on the western trails and are hard to avoid in *Oregon Trail II*. (One exception is at Three Crossings, where you can choose another path.) Otherwise, lessen your chances of getting stuck by forgetting the Conestoga, keeping your wagon load light, and having enough draft animals to pull the wagon's weight.

If you do get stuck, double-team the animals and try to continue. If this doesn't work, you'll need to lighten your load and try double-teaming again. Sometimes you have to lighten your load repeatedly until your animals are finally able to pull the wagon free.

wagon stuck in mud

Some stretches of trail are pretty much always muddy. Others get muddy during or after heavy rains or snow melt. Try to avoid mud in the first place and use the strategies for deep sand if you're stuck.

wagon train morale is low

Although Greenhorns gain or lose points at the end of the game based on wagon train morale, low morale isn't as big a problem for them as it is for Adventurers and Trail Guides. If morale falls too low, an Adventurer is liable to be dismissed from service as wagon train captain and demoted to Greenhorn.

For Trail Guides it's even worse; they can be fired, automatically ending the game. If you're told that wagon train morale is low, you'd best do something quickly. What you do depends on the cause of the low morale.

Resting often helps, but not when supplies are low. If that's the case, hurry to a site where you can restock and rest. If food is low or you're out of meat, fruit, or vegetables, you need to replenish them.

Talking to people also helps boost morale. Get advice from folks; see what they have to say. Pioneers like it when their leaders listen to them. And certain supplies, such as musical instruments and playing cards, raise morale. So do cooking and musical skills.

Finally, if your occupation is pastor, your congregation—er, wagon train—receives a weekly morale boost. But the most important thing by far is to make good decisions so that morale doesn't suffer in the first place.

water poisoning

Pools of poison water dotted the western trails, particularly in the Rocky Mountains and the Great Basin region between the Rockies and the Sierra Nevadas. Drinking poison water can make people and animals sick or even die. But imagine dying of thirst and coming on a suspicious water hole; it's hard not to drink!

What to do? Try to keep good drinking water with you at all times. And if you are poisoned, rest a day or two but don't hang around that water hole too long.

Peppermint helps.

wound

If a person has gangrene and you're forced to amputate the affected limb, he or she is left with a serious wound that must be treated properly in order to avoid further serious complications (as if the gangrene weren't serious enough). Cleaning and dressing the wound, applying sulfur, and using an antiseptic are all good things to do. Resting won't do much good unless one of these three treatments is used first.

Never rub salt in a wound; it's cruel and can have a bad effect on wagon train morale.

"You've been dismissed!"

This can happen if you're an Adventurer guiding the wagon train and morale falls too low. There's really nothing you can do except continue as a Greenhorn, no longer making decisions as to the path to follow. If morale doesn't improve in a few weeks, there's a slim chance you might get another shot as captain, and if this happens, act fast to improve things. Folks will be impatient and won't tolerate much before dismissing you again.

Of course, it's best not to let morale fall too low in the first place.

"You've been fired!"

This is what happens to Trail Guides who let moral fall too low. Sorry, game's over.

Positive Events

Take heart, not everything that happens on the trail is bad. Below are some positive events that can help you on your journey.

abandoned wagon

The sight of an abandoned wagon caused mixed emotions on the trail. It signaled another party's misfortune but meant there could be some useful supplies left behind. Take the time to check an abandoned wagon; you may find something you need. But dump any deadweight. You don't want to lug that grandfather clock or kitchen cabinet around; it's not good for your animals.

abandoned buildings

Abandoned buildings are even more of a mixed blessing than abandoned wagons. On the one hand, if you're counting on that trading post, fort, or mission to buy supplies, but you now find it collapsing into ruins, you're out of luck. But you can still search the ruins with a fair chance of finding something useful (free of charge, no less!). You can also pick up another useless burden doing this, which you'd better dump straight off.

caught some fish

Fish caught in the rivers and lakes along the trail are a welcome addition to your diet. But you'll never catch any if you don't have a fishing pole, net, or spear—the latter especially useful for nabbing spawning salmon in the northwestern rivers. And you'll never catch them if you don't take a rest near a river or lake.

Independence Day

The Fourth of July was an exciting holiday for pioneers. Wagon trains almost always celebrated. When Independence Day rolls around, you should take the opportunity to celebrate, too. It gives a good-sized boost to morale (and lowers morale if you skip it).

wild fruit and wild vegetables

At the right time of year and along certain stretches, you'll find wild fruit and vegetables. Stop to gather them in most cases. You'll lose a half-day's traveling, but you'll end up with a large amount of food (which prevents scurvy). You can save time by gathering while continuing, but you'll get less food for your troubles.

Of course, you can ignore the fruit or vegetables altogether, if you already have plenty, and it won't hurt your morale. It will clobber morale, though, if you need the stuff.

"You've been elected captain!"

If you're an Adventurer, you'll receive this message shortly after setting off. Wagon trains usually didn't elect their captains until they'd been out on the trail a few days. If you accept the position, you'll then be the leader of the wagon train, choosing which path to take at splits in the trail and making other decisions that affect the well-being of those who've put their trust in you.

If you get wet feet and decline the captaincy, you'll automatically be demoted to Greenhorn.

"You've been hired as Trail Guide!"

You receive this message if you've chosen Trail Guide as your level of play. This means folks are paying you to lead them to a new home. When this message comes up, you must accept it or end the game.

The first $500 of your pay is then added to your cash funds, the remaining $1,000 paid when you reach your chosen destination. If you don't lead these good people where they want to go, though, they'll be so upset they'll refuse to pay you that last $1,000 (a blow to your final score).

"You've been re-elected!"

This is an important second chance for a demoted captain. Now you can boost morale, lead the wagon train successfully to your destination, and raise your final score significantly in the process. Don't blow it! If you don't reach your destination within the next few days or at least do something to raise morale, they'll fire you again.

NOTE

Sometimes the best response to an event is a combination of resting and some other course of action. For example, in the case of a snakebite, the best thing to do is to treat the wound using the tourniquet/suction method, followed by a period of rest. Yet once you click the "Use the tourniquet/suction method" button, your choice of options goes away, apparently preventing you from resting. But all you have to do to rest anytime you like is to click once anywhere on the map screen. This allows you to stop on the trail between landmarks, at which time you can indicate how long you wish to rest. *So in our snakebite example, you can choose the tourniquet/suction treatment and then, immediately afterward, click on the map to rest. This works well for any number of events, especially injuries and diseases.*

TIPS FOR SUCCESSFUL HUNTING

Hunting is one of the most popular aspects of *Oregon Trail II*, and while you might not like the notion of killing animals in this day and age, it was a matter of survival for the pioneers. Although it isn't a good idea to rely only on hunting for food, it can save you from going hungry when you lose your supplies or simply run out sooner than expected. So, for this reason, you need to learn how to hunt on the trail.

The terrain, vegetation, and animals you see while hunting change as you travel west, and you won't find buffalo where buffalo didn't live in the mid-1800s. Time of year makes a big difference too—you probably won't see bears in winter.

While you're hunting you might find buffalo, pronghorn antelope, deer, elk (also called "wapiti"), moose, mountain goats, black bears, grizzly bears, squirrels, ground squirrels, rabbits, ducks, and geese. Some of

these animals appear more often than others, just as they did on the western trails.

Be patient when you begin a new hunting scene. Animals won't always appear right away. Wait at least 20 seconds before moving on. After waiting a while, you can sometimes scare game out by firing once. This wastes a bullet, though, and it doesn't always work. And don't forget to reload right away.

If you still can't scare up any dinner, you'll have to try again in a day or two. That's just the way it is. Oh, and never try hunting in the desert: animals won't appear. It's also unwise to hunt in any one place for very long. You'll hunt the area out or scare all the animals away, so keep moving.

Each hunting expedition uses up a day of trail time. If you go hunting on June 1, your next day of travel will be June 2 (or longer if you decide to rest for one or more days after). So too much hunting will slow you down.

You can only take up to 20 bullets or cartridges with you on a hunting expedition, if you have that many left in your supplies. And unlike previous versions of the program, you have to reload your weapon after a shot (that's because there were no automatic weapons in the mid-1800s; even revolvers weren't widely available until the 1860s).

You can't go hunting unless you have firearms and ammunition. A rifle, some bullets, and some gunpowder are part of the basic supplies available at the start of the game. You're welcome to shop for extras, too. Try the gunsmith's, where you'll find rifles, bullets, gunpowder, shotguns, shot, and pistols. Rifles and pistols require bullets, while shotguns use shot. Both need gunpowder. Firing a weapon uses these supplies up, and you also lose them through theft and accidents. Your gunpowder is ruined if it gets wet, so keep an eye out.

If you own only one weapon, you'll automatically hunt with it. But if you own two or three, you'll have to choose one every time you go out. There are advantages and disadvantages to each. Rifles are best for bringing down big game, anything larger than a goose or rabbit. Shotguns are best for squirrels, ground squirrels, rabbits, ducks, and geese, which are more common along the trail but give less meat. Pistols have a short range and are only good if an animal is close to you. Rifles and pistols both require a better aim than shotguns.

Larger animals, especially buffalo, moose, elk, and bears, may take more than one hit to bring them down. And you need to hit them in the right spot. That's why sharpshooting skills are so handy for hunting. Gunsmiths and trappers have sharpshooting skills, too, an ability which gives you several advantages. You're more likely to hit moving game, more likely to kill large game with a single hit, and less likely to suffer an accidental gunshot wound. If you're a trapper, you also have tracking skills, which helps find wild game in the first place.

Hunting carries risks. You can be wounded, attacked and mauled by a dangerous animal (especially buffalo or bear), or sprain or break something during your trek. Sharpshooting skills help avoid these pitfalls, but not entirely. Watch out during a buffalo stampede. No matter what your skills, accidents happen.

Not every animal gives you the same amount of meat. It varies among species, age, and gender. The following table shows how much to expect from each animal hunted in *Oregon Trail II*.

ANIMAL		MINIMUM EDIBLE MEAT (IN LBS.)	MAXIMUM EDIBLE MEAT (IN LBS.)
	buffalo	200	500
	moose	150	350
	grizzly bear	75	300
	elk	100	225
	black bear	50	175
	deer	15	150
	mountain goat	25	115
	pronghorn	20	50
	goose	4	10
	rabbit	1	4
	duck	1	3
	squirrel	1	1
	ground squirrel	1	1

If there's at least one other person in your wagon party (as opposed to the entire wagon train), someone goes out hunting with you. Between the two of you, you can carry 150 to 250 pounds of meat back to your wagon. Not a small feat since your wagon train is a good ways from where you're hunting (otherwise you'd scare the animals away). But this means you can't make a return trip for more meat because scavengers such as coyotes and buzzards will have already made short work of the leftovers. Worse, if you're the last person left in your wagon party, you have to go hunting by yourself and can only carry 75 to 125 pounds back.

Meat spoils. This is especially true of freshly hunted game in hot weather. Don't expect it to last more than a few days. You're in luck if you carried salt with you to preserve your game, in which case it's automatically salted for you.

Pioneers sometimes hunted for sport, killing more than they needed. Players can do this, too, but it isn't wise. Shooting animals you don't need wastes your ammunition and weighs you down. Besides, a hunting expedition uses up time that may prove valuable later on as the winter snows approach. Best to be a responsible hunter.

One more hint. Every time you go hunting, you have the chance of discovering some wild fruit or vegetables. (This occurs as an event after the hunt has ended.) Feel free to gather these and take them back to your wagon. This makes for a successful trip even if you don't fire your weapon.

RAFTING DOWN THE COLUMBIA

afting down the Columbia, which has always been second only to hunting as the most popular feature in *The Oregon Trail*, isn't inevitable in *Oregon Trail II*. Before, in *The Oregon Trail*, you always had the option near the end of your journey of rafting down the Columbia or taking the Barlow Toll Road. Now you won't come anywhere near the Columbia unless you're bound for the Willamette Valley in northern Oregon. So if you want to go rafting, choose either the Willamette Valley (during the early years) or Oregon City (in later years) as your destination at the start of the game.

If you reach The Dalles in the very early years of the simulation, from 1840 to 1845, you'll have no choice but to raft down the river if you want to make it to the Willamette Valley. But you can choose either to raft yourself (which is risky but doesn't cost anything, and is a lot more fun) or hire someone (safer, but expensive).

From 1846 on, there was a third option, the Barlow Toll Road. This will cost around five dollars, depending on the number of draft animals pulling your wagon, but it's much safer than the river, even if it does pose the same dangers as earlier parts of the trail.

The river is a thrill—quick and potentially deadly. To navigate it, use your mouse. Try to avoid rocks and whirlpools so you don't tip and drown (or at the very least lose your supplies). And good luck.

In *Oregon Trail II*, rafting has four segments. One from The Dalles to Cascades Portage, one from Cascades Portage to McCord Creek, one from McCord Creek to Fort Vancouver, and one from Fort Vancouver to the Willamette Valley (later Oregon City).

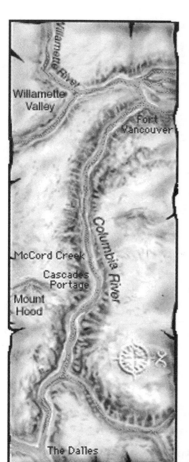

The first section, from The Dalles to Cascades Portage, is difficult but you can make it. Be on guard early for a whirlpool and several rocks. Later, about three-quarters of the way down, you're met by two rocks jammed into a narrow bend in the river. And watch out for a nasty rock that lies near the north (right) bank close to the end.

The second section, from Cascades Portage to McCord Creek, is a stretch of sheer suicide. For this reason, pioneers landed their rafts at Cascades Portage and dragged their supplies around the rapids—a slow, rugged trek of about three miles, but worth it. The author of this book, who is one of the designers of the program and laid out the rocks and whirlpools himself, has never made it through these rapids. In fact, only one member of our design team has negotiated this stretch and lived to tell about it, and that was after two months of trying. Maybe you should walk around like the pioneers did.

If you're still alive, you'll hit the third segment of rapids beginning at McCord Creek. The worst is behind you now. From here to Fort Vancouver it's much like the first stretch, difficult but doable. Several large islands cause temporary splits in the river, and it's not safe to go down some of these divergent paths. But one of the safest paths is, interestingly enough, down a narrow channel that's barely wide enough for your raft. Once here, watch out for the cross-currents.

The final rafting segment begins at Fort Vancouver, which you can visit if you like. From Fort Vancouver your raft will actually leave the Columbia and travel up the Willamette River. This is the easiest stretch of all. You'll notice that your raft behaves differently going upstream, because you're rowing against the current. Sometimes this causes you to go backwards, but at least the current helps you avoid the few rocks and whirlpools you meet. When you reach the end of this stretch, you've made it to the Willamette Valley or Oregon City!

By the way, when you reach The Dalles and before you brave the rapids, save your game. It would be a shame to make it so far only to lose your life in the river! (Wouldn't the pioneers have liked a second chance like that?)

SOME ADDITIONAL HELPFUL HINTS

It's time to spill the beans over a few of the mysteries in *Oregon Trail II*. The hints in this chapter should enlighten you and help you on your way.

Visiting Blacksmiths

Most towns and forts have blacksmiths, and visiting one boosts the staying power of your wagon parts. Wagon parts start out in good condition, but wear on the trail. For this reason, broken parts are likely late in your journey. Visiting a blacksmith always rejuvenates them somewhat (though not completely), so it's a good idea to visit a smith on the trail. Just going into a shop is enough to make repairs.

Visiting Doctors

Most towns and forts have doctors, although they're not always easy to find. In town, doctors' offices are always indicated by a sign such as Physician, Surgeon, or M.D. In forts, however, doctors are usually found behind some closed door with no sign outside.

If you're looking for a doctor at a fort, pass the cursor over the various buildings and closed doors until it changes to the forward arrow, letting you in. You may be able to find a doctor's office this way, and it's always a good idea to try.

When you visit a doctor, *Oregon Trail II* assumes that your wagon party has been able to receive medical attention, thus boosting their health. Sick people are a little more likely to get better, and those who are on the brink of illness are less likely to fall sick.

Getting a Boost to Morale

Wagon train morale is important, especially if you're an Adventurer or Trail Guide. Low morale can get you demoted or fired. Making good decisions is by far the best way to keep morale high, but there are other things you can do.

Talk to people along the way. Each conversation you have improves morale, since people like it when their leader asks questions and listens to their advice. Resting can boost morale as well, as long as you have plenty of supplies, your wagon train isn't behind schedule, and you're not in a dangerous situation (such as stopping in a desert). Just remember not to rest for more than a week, as it makes people feel as if they're stuck in the middle of nowhere with nothing to do.

Understanding Human Nature

You're going to meet a lot of characters in *Oregon Trail II*, nearly 200 of them. Many of them are fellow members of your wagon train, who travel with you wherever you go. Others are people you meet along the way and might not see again. Most of these folks are good, honest, and reasonably intelligent, and it's fun to strike up a conversation with them. But a few aren't so trustworthy.

In fact, a few are downright bad-tempered and best left alone. They are scoundrels, liars, and cheats. Or maybe just basically good people who don't know what they're talking about. This last is something to watch out for. That is, a person can give you good, reliable advice one time and be mistaken another. So don't believe everything everybody tells you.

And don't believe everything you read, either. The Guidebook in *Oregon Trail II* is full of accurate information and good advice. But just as with publications back in the mid-1800s, it's *not always* right. Be a critical observer and judge for yourself the reliability of what you see and hear.

One character in particular to watch out for is Nicholas J. Tillman, whose friends (what few of them there are) call him Nick. He's well-meaning for the most part, but unfortunately he's a fool and a blowhard. Hardly anything he says is believable. In fact, if he advises you to do something, you can be pretty sure you shouldn't do it. (By the way, longtime users of MECC products may recognize the name Nick Tillman from an old MECC Apple II program titled *Zoyon Patrol*, which is set in modern times. *Zoyon Patrol*'s Nick Tillman is the namesake and direct descendant of the character in *Oregon Trail II*. The two Nicks are equally unreliable.)

Nick Tillman
as portrayed by
Wayne Studer

You'll also notice a strong resemblance between Nicholas J. Tillman and another untrustworthy character in *Oregon Trail II*, the hapless fraud Dr. Brogan Cavanaugh. Actually, they're first cousins, as Nick admits in one of his conversations. But this doesn't prove that unreliability is inherited, does it?

Nifty Little Sound Effects and Other Fun Stuff

You can hear nifty sound effects by clicking on various items in certain scenes. Cattle in towns and forts go moo, horses whinny, dogs bark, cats meow, and most people offer some sort of greeting—unless they sneeze, snore, or simply ignore you.

Also, mid-nineteenth-century Americans were notorious for chewing tobacco, a habit that disgusted many European visitors. Nevertheless, spittoons were handy in most public places. Click on a spittoon and you'll hear the appropriate sound effect.

Incidentally, Sutter's Fort is crawling with cats—an in-joke from one of the artists. Some other jokes or bad puns are found on the business signs in several towns.

If you click on a newspaper office or posted newspaper, you'll not only see a headline for that week, but the headline will be automatically recorded in your diary. Clicking on a wanted poster is recorded, too.

Don't overlook the list of credits available through the *About Oregon Trail* command (under the Help menu on Windows, and the Apple menu on the Macintosh). Not everything here is meant to be taken seriously, though, and can be downright silly.

While in the command, if you click once on the pictures on the left side of the screen as the credits are rolling past, you'll see a summary of your current computer hardware setup. This information may come in handy, especially if you need to contact MECC for help on some *Oregon Trail II* problem. (Heaven forbid!) Clicking again on the information will restore the pretty pictures, which are selected at random from the program's huge stock of scenes.

MUSIC IN OREGON TRAIL II

Eric Speier

The music in a movie, television show, and even a computer game is designed to serve as a kind of emotional shorthand for the overall experience. In other words, as you sit in the comfort and safety of your home or a theater enjoying a dramatic presentation, music helps stimulate your emotions so you feel more a part of things. You're in no danger, but dangerous-sounding music lets you sense what's coming.

In short, the music is no accident in *Oregon Trail II*. It heightens the experience, and that's what it's meant to do. Most of the music was composed and performed by Eric Speier, a Los Angeles-based composer who has written music for software, television, and film. Based on notes from the program's designers and additional input from Larry Phenow, the *Oregon Trail II* music co-ordinator, Speier wrote and arranged the music, giving it a strong period feel that evokes a sense of Americana.

The music has dramatic sweep encompassing a range of emotions, expressing epic grandeur, challenge, and bold enterprise. It's also meant to be episodic in nature, with themes that represent certain areas and events along the trail. It was created to loop through a segment for as long as it takes users to get through that segment.

The music falls into two groups: *soundtrack music* taken from the *Oregon Trail II Suite* composed by Speier, and *incidental music* played at certain points along the way, such as towns, forts, and trading posts.

Soundtrack Music

The soundtrack music consists of several parts. The first of these is the "Opening Theme," played while the title screen is visible as well as while you're creating your character and circumstances for the start of the simulation. This theme is meant to create an overall sense of epic adventure. The incidental music for each of the four jumping-off towns is also based on the melody of this theme.

The first segment of the trail features a rollicking, upbeat tune that expresses the lively optimism of emigrants just setting off on their journey. The people and animals are fresh and generally in good health. Unless they didn't make adequate preparations, their wagons are in good condition and they have plenty of supplies. The trail itself is mostly flat and smooth, and the environment is familiar, with plenty of water and vegetation. Unless travelers started out too early or too late, it's springtime. They're generally in good spirits and moving at a steady pace.

Of course, if things aren't going very well for your wagon party, a darker undercurrent will enter the music. The theme will be played with different instruments and/or harmonization to give it an ominous sound. As a result, each trail-segment theme has three moods: "all's well," "some concern," and "rough going." Words on a page aren't adequate to describe these different moods in detail, but once you've played *Oregon Trail II* for a while, you'll recognize these mood swings and understand how they provide you with a constant reminder of your current conditions.

The music for the second segment of the trail begins in the vicinity of Fort Kearny. It slows down, though with its ¾ waltz time signature it still has a positive feel to it. Emigrants have been out on the trail for a few weeks now and the newness of the experience has worn off. Travelers have settled down to a daily routine that rarely changes. The trail is starting to get rougher, steeper, and more difficult. The countryside looks unfamiliar, with strange rock formations cropping up. The climate is changing, too, becoming steadily hotter and drier. But despite all this, most emigrants remain optimistic. Unless they've encountered unusual, unexpected hardships, their general health is good and they still have plenty of supplies. And they're enjoying the wonders of the landscape, often awed by what they see around them.

The third segment of the trail begins just after Fort Laramie. Here the music turns more sedate, dominated by guitar, harmonica, and a whistle. People are fatigued, and some regret they ever started on this journey. They're now in rough, elevated, semi-desert country— usually hot and dry during the day, but often surprisingly cold at night. Supplies may be getting scarce, there's strain on the wagon, and the animals are tiring, too. The trail splits off into various branches. Which way to go? The music here expresses these feelings of fatigue and uncertainty.

The music for the fourth segment of the trail begins as emigrants cross the Rocky Mountains and enter the regions of the Great Basin. This is the most alien country, generally like nothing they've ever seen before. The beat is slow with a steady undercurrent of low strings and minor-key progressions that express the strangeness of the landscape and the potential danger from the mountains and deserts. This is the most difficult stretch of trail. The pioneers are tired, worried, and discouraged. Deaths are more likely here than anywhere else, and the music conveys real foreboding.

By contrast, on the fifth segment of the trail, the tempo picks up again with swooping strings and highly rhythmic percussion. This expresses adventure and anticipation. Emigrants are nearing the end of their journey, and they know it. But some of the most difficult mountains, hills, and rivers yet lie ahead, so there's still an underlying sense of danger.

Rafting down the Columbia has its own special musical theme, dominated by horns and percussion, to relay the danger of the river and the anticipation of journey's end. The grandiose "Concluding Success Theme" actually pops up from time to time during the "Rafting Theme," teasing you with a hint of what lies ahead. It plays in full when you reach your destination.

Other music occurs at special places and times along the way. When you reach the edge of a desert, a quiet, spooky "Desert Theme" plays, conveying both the stillness and the hazards of the trek ahead. This doubles as a "Death Theme," playing when someone in your wagon party dies. When you reach a hill or mountain, you hear the "Hill Theme," expressing the dangers posed by your climb or descent. And when you stop to rest, you hear the "Rest Theme," a peaceful melody based on the opening phrase of the traditional American folk tune "Shenandoah."

Other events also have short musical themes that, because of their brevity, are called *stings*. Several negative stings can be heard when bad things happen (such as a tipped wagon). There's also a positive sting that plays when certain good events occur, such as finding wild vegetables along the trail.

Incidental Music

Then there's the incidental music that plays when you visit a town, fort, or trading post. (But you don't hear this music unless you actually go into the settlement, as opposed to simply arriving there.) The four jumping-off towns (Independence, St. Joseph, Nauvoo, and Kanesville/Council Bluffs) each have their own music based on the opening theme, conveying the overall mood of the town. For instance, the music for Nauvoo, the chief starting point for Mormon pioneers, has a stately, religious feel to it, while the other jumping-off towns convey a wilder mood.

In other towns along the trail you'll hear a wide variety of popular melodies from the mid-1800s. Although you'll always hear the same music in each jumping-off town, you won't always hear the same music in these other towns (except Great Salt Lake City, whose musical theme is based on the traditional Mormon hymn "Come, Come Ye Saints").

These songs are arranged and performed by Eric Speier, Larry Phenow, Glen Anderson, and Mark Stillman, contributors also to the music described below for forts and trading posts. Among the songs played at random in towns are "Oh, Susanna," "Long, Long Ago," "Buffalo Gals," "Go Tell Aunt Nancy," "Camptown Races," and "Skip to My Lou."

Forts have their own sets of random melodies. At military forts, such as Fort Kearny, you'll hear the period songs "Yellow Rose of Texas," "The Campbells Are Coming," and "Yankee Doodle." They're performed in a military style with snare drum, fife, and/or bugle. Non-military forts have a different set of songs played in a "folksier" manner, including "Old Dan Tucker," "Little Liza Jane," "Blue Tail Fly," "Red River Valley," and, again, "Yellow Rose of Texas."

Trading posts boast period melodies with even simpler arrangements: "On Top of Old Smoky," "Wayfarin'

Stranger," "Shenandoah," "Bury Me Not on the Lone Prairie," "Green Grow the Laurels," and others, as well as simplified renditions of some of the songs noted previously for towns and forts.

The two Native American villages in *Oregon Trail II*–Pawnee Village and the Potawatomi Indian Town– feature special recordings of traditional Native American music from the same region and related nations, performed by William Pensoneau.

Thus it's hoped that the music in *Oregon Trail II* provides a sense of adventure (via the "soundtrack") and an appreciation for the actual music of the time and place (via the "incidental music"). And maybe, just maybe, you'll find yourself humming some of those melodies after the CD has been neatly placed back in its jewel box.

LANDMARKS ALONG THE TRAIL

Notes on Specific Landmarks

There are nearly 250 landmarks—natural features, towns, forts, trading posts, and the like—in *Oregon Trail II*. Some are simply intriguing places, such as Chimney Rock, that pioneers took note of as interesting sights or guideposts on their journey. Others were significant to emigrants for more practical reasons. And still others changed from year to year, giving pioneers either a pleasant or unpleasant surprise. Below are notes on specific sites along the trail, followed by a complete list of landmarks.

The Main Oregon Trail from Independence, Missouri

Independence   This was the first and most popular of the jumping-off towns where pioneers gathered to plan their journey, buy supplies, and form wagon trains.

Blue River   A free bridge was built here in 1859, permitting an easy crossing. Before that, the river had to be forded or floated.

Westport   An early town on the trail. If you quickly realize that you've forgotten some important supplies, or lost supplies crossing the Blue River, go into town and do some shopping.

New Santa Fe   Another early town. If you didn't find what you needed in Westport, maybe you'll find it here.

Lawrence   This town didn't spring up along the trail until 1854.

Topeka   Another town founded in 1854.

Kansas River   A ferry was established here in 1844. Before then you had no choice but to ford or float.

Saint Mary's Mission

A mission to the local Indians established in 1848. There's a trading post here, so you can stop and buy supplies if you like.

Red Vermillion River

Potawatomi chief Louis Vieux ran a toll bridge here beginning in 1848.

St. Joseph Road Junction

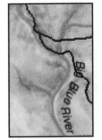

In 1843, a split in the trail appeared here. You'll almost certainly want to take the Oregon Trail heading west. But if you're dangerously low on supplies, it may be worth your while to head toward St. Joseph. It's out of your way, but you can restock there or at one of the trading posts along the way, depending on the year. (Early on, there are no trading posts around here.)

Hollenberg Ranch

A trading post was established here in 1857.

Rock Creek Station

Another place where you can buy supplies, also established in 1857.

Thirty-two Mile Station

This supply station didn't appear until 1859.

Fort Kearny

A major landmark established in 1848. Not only was it an important point for stocking up on supplies, but it also signaled the end of the first part of the journey on the main Oregon Trail. After this, the trail got rougher.

Midway Station

Established in 1859. Some supplies available.

South Platte River

A very wide but often shallow river crossing that offers no alternatives but to ford or float. Watch out for quicksand.

California Hill

The first major hill on the main Oregon Trail. Not especially steep going up, but a change for emigrants who, up until this point, were accustomed to level road.

Windlass Hill   Shortly after going up California Hill, wagons had to go down Windlass Hill, which was a little more dangerous. It wasn't too difficult compared to the steeper hills out west, but it could prove tragic to careless pioneers.

Chimney Rock

There's nothing special about Chimney Rock except that it's one of the most striking landmarks on the trail. It was such an impressive sight and considered such a milestone that nearly every emigrant diary mentioned it.

Robidoux Pass/Mitchell Pass   Until 1853, wagon trains had little choice but use Robidoux Pass to detour the impassable Scotts Bluff. In 1848, Robidoux Pass Trading Post was established here. It was abandoned in 1853 after the opening of Mitchell Pass, a shorter path through the Scotts Bluff area.

Laramie River   A ferry operated here beginning in 1847. It was replaced by a toll bridge in 1852.

Fort William/ Fort John/Fort Laramie   From the earliest days of the trail, a fort lay just on the other side of the Laramie River. At first it was called Fort William. In 1842 it was changed to Fort John. A trail split appeared here in 1847 with the Mormon Trail coming in from the northeast. Finally, in 1849, the fort's name was officially changed to Fort Laramie, which is what people had been calling it informally for years.

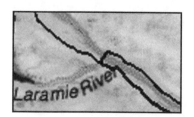

Whatever its name, this is an important place for resting and restocking supplies. When you continue, be sure to take the Oregon Trail heading west—that is, unless you want to travel back east.

North Platte River

This river crossing underwent quite a few changes through the years. Until 1847 you had no choice but to ford or float across. In that year, however, a ferry was established. In 1852, the ferry was replaced by a toll bridge. The last change occurred in 1859, when a free bridge was built, providing a quick and easy crossing to everyone.

Mormon Ferry Trading Post

Located a short ways past the North Platte crossing, this trading post was established in mid-1847.

Independence Rock

Second only to Chimney Rock as a major natural landmark, its name gives a clue to its importance as a gauge of trail progress. If wagon trains reached Independence Rock on or before Independence Day (July 4), they knew they were on schedule and should have little trouble reaching their destination before winter. But if they reached it after July 4, they were running behind and needed to push harder to catch up.

Incidentally, emigrants would often carve their names in the rock (as they would at certain other points along the trail), an historical fact that's alluded to in some of the characters' conversations but is otherwise irrelevant.

Three Crossings

This site marked a brief split in the trail that offered pioneers two choices, each of which carried risks. If they took the Three Crossings Route, they had to follow a narrow, rugged path that crossed the Sweetwater River three times in a row. If they took the Deep Sand Route, they only had to cross the river once (until later on the trail), but had to pass through a stretch of trail notorious for its thick, heavy sand that could sometimes turn to quicksand after heavy rains.

It's best that you take the Deep Sand Route. It's pretty safe unless there's been rain recently, and even then you'll only risk losing a draft animal to quicksand and not much else. Each and every river crossing, however, carries the risk of losing supplies, people, and animals.

Sweetwater River Crossings

Depending on which road you take, you'll have either three or just one crossing of the Sweetwater River immediately after Three Crossings. Usually the river is shallow enough to ford, but be sure to check the conditions; sometimes it's just deep enough to make fording a bad idea.

Ice Spring Slough

The two different paths link together again at Ice Spring Slough. Unless for some reason you want to turn around and head back, you'll always want to take the road to South Pass.

Rocky Ridge

A rugged uphill climb. Be careful.

Lander Trading Post

Frederick Lander established a trading post and supply point along the Oregon Trail in 1854. Several years later, in 1858, he completed work on a shortcut to Fort Hall that bypassed Fort Bridger, creating a trail split at the site of his trading post. This shortcut was known as the Lander Cutoff.

The Lander Cutoff can definitely shave time off your journey, so if you're running late in 1858 or later, you might consider it. But the cutoff does hold risks. It's a very rugged road offering either no water or bad water for the most part. (You'd better skip it if you don't have a canteen or, better yet, a water keg.) Travel as quickly as you can, either 10 or 12+ hours per day, although this increased pace can cause accidents on such a rough trail.

Final Sweetwater River Crossing

If you stay on the main trail after the Lander Cutoff, you'll once again reach the Sweetwater River. After crossing it this time, you'll leave it behind for good. As before, fording is usually but not always the best way to cross. Check the conditions before deciding!

South Pass

Like Chimney Rock and Independence Rock, South Pass was important only as a landmark to travelers, offering the easiest way across the Continental Divide. In fact, its incline was so broad and gradual it was hard to believe you were crossing the Rocky Mountains. It also marked the halfway point of the journey and the extreme edge of the Oregon Country (definitely not the edge of the modern state of Oregon, which was still many hundreds of miles away).

Dry Sandy Trading Post

A trading post was established in 1859 at the landmark known as Dry Sandy.

"Parting of the Ways"

Rocky Mountains

This location got its name from the fact that, beginning in 1844, it was often the site of wagon train splits, with one group taking the Sublette Cutoff, bound for Fort Hall and Oregon, and the other heading toward Fort Bridger and California. This wasn't, however, the only or even most frequently used place where the trails to Oregon and California split; that would come farther on, at the California Trail Junction.

Note that not all Oregon pioneers took the rugged Sublette Cutoff, especially those eager to buy fresh supplies, since Fort Bridger is closer at this point than Fort Hall.

Green River

This, the more southerly of the two Green River crossings in *Oregon Trail II*, is on the main trail, on the way to Fort Bridger. (The other crossing is farther north, on the Sublette Cutoff.) In addition to the standard methods of fording or floating, Shoshoni Indians are usually available to help you across if you're willing to trade for their services. (The Indians may not, however, always be there, particularly in winter.)

These Indians might accept your offer of certain items of interest to them (animals, clothing, blankets, firearms, ammunition, some foods, etc.) roughly equivalent to ten dollars in value. Don't haggle with them too much; like most traders in *Oregon Trail II* they'll lose patience and start making greater demands. At any rate, hiring Indians to help you cross the river decreases the odds of an accident. In mid-1847, a ferry was established at this crossing, offering another safe option.

Blacks Fork Bend/Fort Bridger

This was the traditional site of an annual traders' rendezvous; it was also a point where the trail split, with one road (the Salt Lake Alternate) heading toward the Great Salt Lake Valley, offering a shortcut to California. The other road was the main Oregon Trail, which headed north toward Fort Hall.

In 1841, Fort Bridger was built at Blacks Fork Bend and quickly became an important supply point for wagon trains. Fort Bridger operated until September 28, 1857, when it was burned and abandoned during a scuffle between the Mormons and the U.S. government. In mid-spring the following year, 1858, the army built a new fort on the same site. This rebuilt fort was known as New Fort Bridger.

West End of the Sublette Cutoff

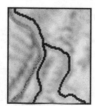

This is where the Sublette Cutoff, established in 1844, linked back up with the main Oregon Trail. Unwary travelers might take a wrong turn here and find themselves headed back where they came from. Be sure to continue on the road to Fort Hall.

Thomas Fork

This rather small river could be surprisingly treacherous, especially after heavy rain or snow melt. A toll bridge was built here in 1853. If you can afford the toll, it's well worth the price.

Big Hill

Big Hill was, as its name implies, a steep descent. Don't continue down without using some means of braking your wagon.

Smith's Trading Post

A mountain man named Thomas Smith, nicknamed "Peg-Leg," established a trading post on the road to Fort Hall in 1848. This welcome supply point was abandoned only a couple of years later.

Soda Springs

Another landmark of no great strategic importance except that it made for a fine resting place. But pioneers were often quite impressed by the natural alkaline springs.

Sheep Rock

A large natural formation that had no special importance until 1849, when the alternate road known as Hudspeth Cutoff was established here. Hudspeth Cutoff bypassed Fort Hall and linked up to the California Trail, so California-bound wagons that weren't in need of supplies sometimes took it. But since Fort Hall represents the last really good point for buying supplies for many hundreds of miles, it isn't necessarily the wisest decision to turn off the main trail here. And unless you're going to California or southern Oregon (the Rogue River Valley/Jacksonville), it makes no sense whatsoever.

West End of the Lander Cutoff

This is where the Lander Cutoff, established in 1858, linked back up with the main trail. Be careful not to take a wrong turn here; stay on the road to Fort Hall.

Fort Hall An excellent place to rest and restock supplies. This is especially true if you're going someplace other than northern Oregon (the Willamette Valley/Oregon City) because the next town or fort on the California Trail is roughly 500 miles away.

Raft River Continuing on the Oregon Trail, you'll soon reach the more northerly of the two Raft River crossings. (There's also a third site, even farther south, where you approach the Raft River but don't cross.) You must choose whether to ford or float, with the best decision, as always, depending on the river's current conditions.

California Trail Junction 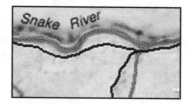 This is your last chance to choose between continuing on the Oregon Trail or splitting off onto the California Trail. If you're going to the Willamette Valley/Oregon City, follow the Oregon Trail. If you're going anywhere else, take the California Trail.

Rock Creek Gorge A rugged descent down to the banks of Rock Creek. Take it easy.

Rock Creek Usually not a difficult crossing.

Three Islands 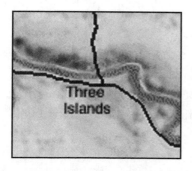 Not to be confused with Three Crossings, this is where the trail split into the main Oregon Trail, which continued toward Fort Boise, and what was known as the South Alternate Route, which bypassed the fort.

The chief advantage of the South Alternate Route is that it avoids crossing the Snake River—not once, but twice—which is often dangerous. There are pros and cons to each decision, and you might experiment with both paths to decide which one you prefer. But if you're in need of supplies, the direct road to Fort Boise is best.

Snake River   If, at Three Islands, you decide to take the road to Fort Boise, you'll immediately come to the first of the two Snake River crossings. This is an interesting crossing because, if the water's low enough to allow fording, wagons can use the three large islands as stepping stones to cross the river. (Yes, given the name, you might guess that three islands would figure into the story somehow.) But remember, never try fording if the river is more than two-and-a-half feet deep.

Fort Boise   This fort was an important supply point along the trail until 1854, when it was abandoned in the wake of badly deteriorating relations with the local Indians.

Final Snake River Crossing   Ferry service began here in 1852, but was given up just two years later, in 1854, as a result of the same difficulties that forced the abandonment of nearby Fort Boise.

East Cow Hollow

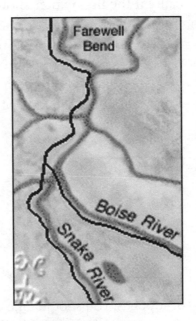

This is where the South Alternate Route joins back up with the main Oregon Trail. Be careful not to take a wrong turn; take the road to Farewell Bend. (If, however, you reach this site from the South Alternate Route, are badly in need of supplies, and it's before 1854, you may want to take the road to Fort Boise, where you can stock up.)

Malheur River   Usually a very easy crossing.

Farewell Bend   Just another milestone to pioneers. It was here that they said "farewell" to the Snake River.

Grande Ronde Valley   The beautiful Grande Ronde Valley was a welcome sight, and might have convinced some to stop and settle here were it not for the fact that the Willamette Valley was even better. At this point your wagon train descends into the valley and you'll have to decide the best way to navigate the downhill path.

Grande Ronde River   Another easy crossing—at least most of the time.

Blue Mountains   The Blue Mountains evoked mixed feelings in the west-ward emigrants. They were a beautiful sight, and their thickly forested slopes gave the pioneers their first glimpse of rich vegetation in a long while. On the other hand, they were a difficult obstacle to overcome, especially if the first winter snows had arrived.

As always when you come to an uphill climb, you have to decide the best way to continue. Double-teaming is often a good idea.

Emigrant Hill   A descent out of the Blue Mountains region. Generally not too difficult.

Doe Canyon   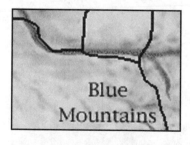 Up until 1855, this is where the trail split be-tween the road to Fort Walla Walla and the Umatilla Shortcut, which headed directly for The Dalles. If you have plenty of supplies, you should take the Umatilla Shortcut. Otherwise, use the Fort Walla Walla Road. In 1855, Fort Walla Walla was abandoned, and the Fort Walla Walla Road was, for all intents and purposes, closed.

Whitman Mission

This was a famous Methodist mission in operation until November 29, 1847, when an Indian attack forced its abandonment. Until then, it was a source of supplies and medical care for many travelers.

Fort Walla Walla

Another major supply point. The fort was abandoned in 1855, and wagon trains stopped traveling this section.

Trail Junction at the Umatilla River

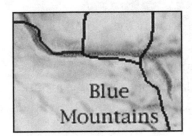

This is where the Fort Walla Walla Road (which closed in 1855, eliminating this junction) linked back up to the more direct Umatilla Shortcut. It can be confusing, so be careful not to make a wrong turn. Unless you're desperately in need of supplies, take the road to The Dalles. Those who took the Umatilla Shortcut—which was everyone after the closing of the Fort Walla Walla Road—crossed the usually shallow Umatilla River at this point.

McDonald Ford of the John Day River

As its name suggests, fording was the most common—but not always the best—way of crossing this river. A ferry was established here in 1858, offering a safer means of crossing.

Deschutes River

Ferry service started here in 1853, ceased in 1855, and resumed in 1858.

Deschutes Hill

Immediately after crossing the river, wagons had to go up another hill. As always, take care to choose the best method.

The Dalles/ Camp Drum/ Camp Dalles

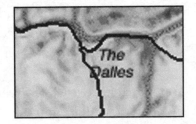

This site signals that your journey is near an end. Up until 1846, those who wanted to get to the Willamette Valley had no choice but to travel down the

Columbia River. Those who could afford it often hired professionals (usually Indians or French trappers) to guide their rafts. Others rafted themselves.

In 1846 the Barlow Toll Road was opened, creating a trail split with the option of traveling a land route to the valley for a relatively small fee. A U.S. Army installation, Camp Drum, was established at The Dalles in 1850. Its name was changed to Camp Dalles three years later, in 1853.

Rafting down the Columbia

Cascades Portage

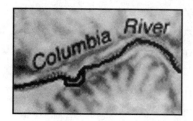

For those who chose to raft down the Columbia, the first major landmark was Cascades Portage. Here they had to decide whether to shoot the rapids or play it safe with the brief but difficult land route leading around. Nearly everyone took the land route since the rapids were sheer suicide.

It's the same way in *Oregon Trail II*. Take the land route if you want to survive. But if you're especially adventurous and want to take your chances, at least follow this advice: Save your game before shooting the rapids. (In fact, it's probably a good idea to save it back at The Dalles, just in case the easier first stretch of river proves too much for you.) That way, when you're killed (as you almost certainly will be), you can go back and try again—and again, and again if you like, until you get tired and finally decide to swallow your pride.

If you do somehow make it through the rapids, you've accomplished a pretty amazing achievement!

McCord Creek

After going around the rapids by land—or miraculously making it through—you'll come to McCord Creek. It's safe to raft again now; the rapids are behind you.

Fort Vancouver

You'll reach Fort Vancouver after the third river segment. If you like, you can stop here to rest, explore, and talk to people. You can even buy supplies, although you probably won't need them. Your destination is just one landmark away.

By the way, the final rafting segment is no longer downstream on the Columbia River. It's going upstream on the Willamette River. The Willamette is much less difficult than the Columbia, but since you're rowing against the current, your raft will behave in a somewhat different manner.

Willamette Valley/Oregon City   You've made it! If you arrive after 1841, you'll find the town of Oregon City nestled comfortably in its beautiful valley. Congratulations!

The Barlow Toll Road

Of course, you may have chosen not to raft down the Columbia. If you decide to take the Barlow Toll Road (available from 1846 on), the first thing you'll have to do is pay the toll, which varies somewhat depending on how many wagons and draft animals you have.

Devil's Half Acre   A short but steep uphill climb that got its name from the fact that it gave emigrants a "devil" of a time. You may be able to climb this hill without using ropes or chains, but they're probably your best bet, especially if the soil is muddy or icy.

Laurel Hill   A downhill version of Devil's Half Acre, only worse. Again, use ropes or chains—if you have them.

Sandy River Toll Bridge   A toll bridge only 17 miles east of Oregon City. In fact, it's the last landmark along the Barlow Toll Road before you reach your destination. The toll is pretty cheap, just fifty cents. But unlike other toll bridges, you have no choice but to pay if you want to cross the river. The banks are so dangerously steep and rocky that fording and floating aren't options.

If you're so broke that you don't have fifty cents, you can probably trade with somebody to get the money you need, though it may take a number of attempts. (Fifty cents was a lot more money in the 1800s than it is today! If you doubt it, go back and look at the price of supplies in the stores along the trail. Fifty cents could buy quite a bit back then.)

The St. Joseph Road

St. Joseph   The St. Joseph Road was a brief stretch of trail leading from the jumping-off town of St. Joseph, Missouri, beginning in 1843. It linked up with the main Oregon Trail after crossing the Big Blue River.

Missouri River   This was the first obstacle for wagon trains setting off from St. Joseph. This river is always much too deep to ford, so you'll need to caulk and float or, better yet, take a ferry. Of course, if the river's frozen, you can chance crossing the ice.

Kennekuk Station   A supply station established in 1858. If you bought adequate supplies in St. Joseph, you probably don't need to stop here unless you lost some supplies while crossing the river.

Walnut Creek   Emigrants along the St. Joseph Road had to cross this small tributary of the Missouri River. A free bridge was built in 1848, so from that year on you no longer have to stop here and decide how to cross.

Big Muddy Station   Another supply station, this one established in 1859.

Vermillion River   Sometimes referred to as Vermillion Creek, this river is usually too deep to ford except during dry spells. No bridges or ferries were established here during the period covered by *Oregon Trail II*, so floating is generally your best bet.

Guittard's Station   Yet another supply station established in 1859.

Marysville, Kansas   A town founded in 1851, not to be confused with the California town named Marysville, which is also in *Oregon Trail II*. A good place for stocking up on supplies.

Big Blue River   A different crossing site than the one located along the main Oregon Trail. A ferry was established here in 1849 by Frank Marshall (who was, incidentally, the founder of nearby Marysville, which he named for his wife). It's a good idea to take this ferry if you can afford it. This river can be treacherous, especially after spring rains and snow melts.

Delays are also common here. The St. Joseph Road Junction, where this stretch joins the main Oregon Trail, is just a short ways past the crossing. There you'll take the Oregon Trail heading west.

The Lander Cutoff

The Lander Cutoff was established in 1858 at the site of the Lander Trading Post as a shortcut along the Oregon Trail. While it did shave quite a few miles off the main trail and offered a shortcut to Fort Hall, it had several drawbacks. For one thing, it was more rugged than the main trail. It was also extremely dry, the only sources of good water being an occasional river or stream. Don't attempt it unless you have a canteen or, better yet, a water keg. Otherwise you or some members of your party may die of thirst along the way. Even with a canteen or water keg, you should increase your pace from the usual eight to ten or more hours per day. Best not to stick around long in this dry region, although the pace will increase the odds of a wagon accident.

Big Sandy Creek This is a good source of water and so a good resting place along the Lander Cutoff. You must cross before continuing. Choose fording or floating depending on the current water depth, which can fluctuate widely.

New Fork River A tributary of the more southerly Green River, this crossing site offers another good source of water and, if needed, a place to rest.

Terrace Canyon You climb uphill through this rugged canyon. If you've been traveling at an increased pace up to now, you may want to return to your normal eight hours per day. Double-teaming is a good way to negotiate the eight-mile stretch of canyon trail.

Nearly 70 miles beyond the edge of the canyon lies the West End of the Lander Cutoff, where you link back up to the main trail. At that point you'll almost certainly want to take the Road to Fort Hall.

The Sublette Cutoff

The Sublette Cutoff, beginning at "Parting of the Ways," was blazed in 1844 as a shortcut that bypassed Fort Bridger on the way to Fort Hall. It offered a shorter route than the main trail, but was somewhat longer than the Lander Cutoff. Similarly, it wasn't nearly as dry as the Lander Cutoff, but was drier than the main trail. In general, if you have plenty of supplies and don't need to rush to Fort Bridger to stock up, the Sublette Cutoff is a good option. If you have a canteen or water keg, you can probably travel at the usual pace of eight hours a day, but if you don't, pick up the pace to 12 or more hours despite the increased risk of wagon accidents.

Green River A ferry was established here, at the more northerly of the two Green River crossings, in 1849. Despite the expense, taking this ferry is a wise investment because the river's standard depth makes fording all but impossible, and even caulking and floating is riskier than usual.

If you need a rest, do so before crossing; this river is the best source of water along the Sublette Cutoff. Fifty-some miles beyond the river, the path links back up with the main trail at the West End of the Sublette Cutoff. Be sure to take the Road to Fort Hall.

The South Alternate Route

For those who didn't want to cross the Snake River at Three Islands and were willing to bypass Fort Boise, the South Alternate Route of the Oregon Trail was a good option.

Bruneau Sand Dunes

These are the largest inland sand dunes in the continental United States. Not surprisingly, the surrounding region is extremely sandy. You may find yourself stuck in deep sand, especially if your wagon is overloaded. (Usually that's not a problem this late on the trail, however.)

Bruneau River

Generally an easier, shallower crossing than the Snake. But the surrounding area is quite rugged, so be careful.

Sinker Creek Butte

This landmark signals the start of an uphill trail. Unless the weather or trail conditions are bad, double-teaming is a good idea.

Givens Hot Springs

A good place to rest. Roughly 50 miles farther on, the South Alternate Route links back up with the main trail at East Cow Hollow. Unless you're low on supplies, follow the Road to Farewell Bend. The Road to Fort Boise is a good option if you need supplies, but that sends you in the wrong direction. In order to head on to the Willamette Valley, you'll have to turn around at the fort once your shopping's done.

By the way, don't bother going to Fort Boise after 1853; it was abandoned. So even if you're low on supplies, go ahead and take the road to Farewell Bend if it's 1854 or later.

The Mormon Trail

Nauvoo

If you jump-off from Nauvoo, Illinois, you'll be traveling the Mormon Trail, which was blazed during the years 1846–47. Many ferries were established at river crossings along the Mormon Trail. Mormons were allowed to use most of them free of charge, but others had to pay.

Oregon Trail II determines whether you're a Mormon based on your chosen destination. If you're going to

Great Salt Lake City, you are, in effect, a Mormon, and Mormon ferries are free. If you're headed anywhere else, you're not.

Mississippi River

Despite this river's depth, it poses no real threat since a free ferry (that is, free to everybody) is always available unless the water's frozen. Still, caulking and floating is a viable option (though not quite as safe as the ferry). Fording, however, is out of the question.

Des Moines River

A ferry is usually available here. It's not free, but it does offer the best means of crossing. Usually this river is much too deep to ford.

Garden Grove Waystation

The Mormons set up this supply station in 1846, and it continued in operation throughout the 1850s.

Mount Pisgah Waystation

This Mormon waystation was established in 1846, but ceased operation after 1852 when it was no longer a landmark on the trail.

Middle Nodaway River

Again, if you can afford it, the ferry provides the safest crossing.

Indian Town

A Potawatomi Indian village along the Mormon Trail. You may be able to trade with some of the Indians here for food or other useful goods.

Kanesville/ Council Bluffs

Kanesville served as an alternate jumping-off town for travelers on the Mormon Trail. If you started at Nauvoo, it's a good place to check your supplies and restock. In 1854 the town was renamed Council Bluffs.

Kanesville Crossing of the Missouri River

Even after Kanesville became Council Bluffs, the nearby Missouri River crossing site continued to be called the Kanesville Crossing. The Mormons established a ferry here in early April 1847. Before then, wagons had to caulk and float or, if the river was frozen, cross the ice. Because of the river's depth, fording is not a good idea.

Winter Quarters/ Florence

The Mormon pioneers who founded Winter Quarters in 1846 spent the remainder of the year here, waiting until spring to continue over the trail. In fact, there is no Mormon Trail beyond Winter Quarters until April 1847. If you arrive here before then, you must wait until

April 1847 before you can continue. (Because of pioneer cooperation and the supplies available at Winter Quarters, you'll use up only a month's supplies during your layover.)

If you arrive in April 1847 or later, you'll be able to continue on your way whenever you like. In late 1848, the Mormons abandoned Winter Quarters for good. The Winter Quarters site remained little more than a group of vacant, deteriorating shacks until 1854, when the town of Florence was founded here.

Elkhorn River Although the Mormon emigrants crossed this river in 1847, they didn't get around to establishing a ferry until the following year.

Pawnee Village Another permanent Indian settlement, this one was the home of members of the Pawnee nation. They viewed the wagon trains with more trepidation than the Potawatomis encountered earlier on the trail, so you may or may not be able to find someone willing to trade with you.

Loup River A Mormon ferry was established here in 1849, offering the best means of crossing.

Deep Ravines Traveling along the north bank of the Platte River, Mormon pioneers found a very rough stretch of trail notorious for rattlesnakes. Snakebites are more likely in this region than anywhere else on the western trails.

Sandy Bluffs At this point the Mormon Trail passes through the well-known Sand Hills region of present-day Nebraska. You may find yourself stuck in deep sand, especially if your wagon is overloaded.

Ancient Bluffs Another very sandy stretch of trail follows.

Chimney Rock Vista   Although Chimney Rock sat on the main Oregon Trail on the south side of the North Platte River, this was the spot where travelers on the Mormon Trail, on the north side of the river, could get a distant view of the famous landmark.

North Platte River   This crossing is just north of Fort Laramie, where the Mormon Trail joins up with the main Oregon Trail. Ferry service was available here from 1847 on. Once you arrive at the fort, be sure to take the Oregon Trail heading west.

The Salt Lake Alternate Route

Once they reached Black Forks Bend (later Fort Bridger), emigrants bound for the Great Salt Lake Valley took what was sometimes known as the Salt Lake Alternate Route. In later years, this was the final, most westerly segment of the Mormon Trail. And in *Oregon Trail II*, it's one of the most dangerous routes. Not only is it extremely rugged, with many hills, mountains, and canyons, but much of it is also very dry. It's probably not wise to take it unless you have a canteen or, preferably, a water keg.

Bear River   Mormons established a ferry here in 1847. Though sometimes shallow enough to ford, this river can be treacherous, so take the ferry.

Weber River   A ferry was established here in 1847. It continued in service until 1858, when it was replaced by a free bridge—which eliminates the need for a decision here.

Pratt's Pass Canyon   Prepare for an uphill climb through the canyon, not as difficult as some that follow. Double-teaming usually works.

Dixie Hollow   A downhill segment, not particularly dangerous.

Little Dutch Hollow

An uphill segment much like Pratt's Pass Canyon.

Big Mountain Descent

Another downhill path, this one is a little more dangerous than Dixie Hollow.

Emigration Canyon Quarantine Station

Established by the Mormons in 1853 in what had previously been called Last Creek Canyon (that is, the last creek before the Salt Lake Valley), this station was not built to provide supplies. Instead, it was used to inspect people and animals for contagious diseases before letting them into the thriving valley.

If anyone in your wagon party (including your animals) is suffering from one of the quarantined diseases, such as measles or smallpox, you'll have to rest here under medical care (click the *Rest here awhile* button) until the illness passes—that is, unless you decide to turn around and go in the opposite direction, but that's not recommended.

Steep Hill/ Donner Hill

This steep climb was the last major obstacle that early emigrants had to face before reaching the Great Salt Lake Valley. The Donner Party had tremendous difficulty struggling up this hill in 1846. (Double-teaming your animals may be sufficient to get you over, although bad weather or soil conditions make ropes or chains more practical.)

By the middle part of the following year, the site was known as Donner Hill. The first band of Mormon emigrants, however, blazed a new path around it in July 1847. From that time on, the terrible obstacle served only as a landmark.

Great Salt Lake Valley/ Great Salt Lake City

The earliest travelers on the Salt Lake Alternate Route passed through the Great Salt Lake Valley, only stopping to rest for a short while. Their path to Oregon or California passed east and then north of the Great Salt Lake itself. This route was known as the Salt Lake Cutoff

(described below). In 1845, Lansford Hastings established a shortcut to California that passed south of the
lake and then headed through the Great Salt Lake
Desert. This was known as the Hastings Cutoff (also
described below).

After the first group of Mormon pioneers, led by
Brigham Young, entered the Great Salt Lake Valley in
late July 1847, they settled down and founded Great
Salt Lake City. (The name wasn't shortened to Salt Lake
City until later.)

Great Salt Lake City quickly became a thriving frontier metropolis, and a rest-stop for wagons heading west.
Emigrants stocked up on supplies here, sometimes ex-
changing their tired draft animals for fresh ones. In fact,
Mormon entrepreneurs earned good profits and performed a valuable service by taking old animals as
trade-ins for fresh ones, nursing them back to health,
and then trading or selling them again.

If Great Salt Lake City is your destination, choose
the *Settle here* option at this point to end the game
successfully. If you reach here after 1844 but Salt Lake
City isn't your destination, you must choose which road
to take: the Salt Lake Cutoff or the Hastings Cutoff. If
you're going to the Willamette Valley (Oregon City),
take the Salt Lake Cutoff. If you're going to the

Sacramento Valley of California or the Rogue River Valley (Jacksonville) of southern Oregon, either trail will lead you there.

Historically, most wagon trains took the longer but less risky Salt Lake Cutoff. The Hastings Cutoff is shorter, but takes you through the Great Salt Lake Desert. *Don't even think of it unless you have a water keg among your supplies!* Without one, you have little chance of making it across this desolate, 70-mile-wide desert. (For more information about crossing the desert, see Hastings Cutoff below.)

The California Trail

The California Trail broke off from the Oregon Trail after crossing the Raft River in what is today south-central Idaho. The place came to be known as the California Trail Junction, and from here the road continued southwest to California.

West End of the Hudspeth Cutoff

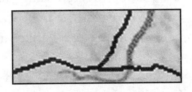

Beginning in 1849, a shortcut named for trailblazer Benoni M. Hudspeth linked up with the main California Trail about 20 miles southwest of the California Trail Junction. When you reach this point, be sure to take the California Trail. Otherwise you'll be heading back east.

City of Rocks

A prominent natural landmark, often mentioned in diaries, and the start of a very rough section of trail.

Salt Lake Cutoff Junction

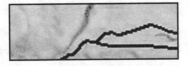

This is where the Salt Lake Cutoff, coming southeast from the Great Salt Lake Valley, joined up with the California Trail. Unless you're bound for Great Salt Lake City, stay on the California Trail.

Granite Mountain

An uphill climb. Double-teaming will usually suffice.

Granite Mountain Pass

At this point you start going down the mountain path. Be sure to brake or anchor your wagon.

North Fork of Mary's River/ North Fork of the Humboldt River

This small tributary is usually shallow enough to ford—but make sure you check the current conditions. Note that after 1844, Mary's River was renamed the Humboldt River.

Emigrant Pass

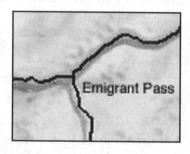

Beginning in 1845, this is where the Hastings Cutoff linked up with the main California Trail. Be sure to choose the California Trail when you're ready to move on.

Gravelly Ford of Mary's River/Gravelly Ford of the Humboldt River

This is another crossing that's nearly always shallow enough to ford. But be careful! The small, smooth pebbles lining the banks and riverbed can make the crossing difficult.

Again, after 1844, Mary's River changed to the Humboldt River.

French Ford Trading Post

An important supply point on the Humboldt. Before this trading post was built in 1850, there was no place to restock supplies for 700 miles (between Fort Hall, Fort Bridger, or Great Salt Lake City to the east, and Johnson's Ranch or Sutter's Fort to the west)—some of the roughest, driest country on the trails.

The fact that the French Ford Trading Post sat halfway across this expanse was no accident; often it was a life-saver. You're out of luck if you're traveling before 1850, but from that year on, be sure to check your supplies when you get here and stock up if necessary. It'll be your last chance for a long while.

Applegate Cutoff/ Lassen's Meadows

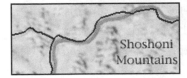

Opened in 1846, the Applegate Cutoff split from the California Trail and headed northwest toward southern Oregon. When you reach this point, take the California Trail if you're going to California (that makes sense), but take the Applegate Road if you're bound for Oregon's Rogue River Valley (later the town of Jacksonville).

Whichever way you go, there are deserts ahead, and your draft animals are going to need something to eat. If you're planning on taking the California Trail, you'll have other opportunities to gather hay for your animals. But if you're going to take the Applegate Road, this is your last chance. In 1848 the popular name for this site changed to Lassen's Meadows.

Big Meadows

If at Applegate Cutoff/Lassen's Meadows you decided to continue on the California Trail, Big Meadows is your last chance to gather hay for your animals before the desert ahead. You had best take advantage of this opportunity.

Mary's Sink/ Humboldt Sink

Mary's River (the Humboldt River as of 1845, when this landmark became Humboldt Sink) has no outlet to the ocean. Rather, it forms a large, stagnant lake and "sinks" into the basin terrain. This site took on added importance in 1848 as the junction of a split in the California Trail.

One path, the Truckee Route (which was the older, main California Trail) passed north of Lake Tahoe, while the newer road, the Carson Route (named for Kit Carson), passed south of the lake. Each route has its advantages and disadvantages, although the Carson Route is probably best once it's available. Both routes, however, cut through the Forty Mile Desert and over the Sierra Nevadas.

The Truckee Route
(The Main California Trail)

This is the main California Trail beyond Mary's Sink/ Humboldt Sink. Before 1848 it was the only trail to California. After 1848, as other roads opened up, it was known as the Truckee Route.

Forty Mile Desert

Ideally, you've gathered hay for your animals at Big Meadows or the earlier Applegate Cutoff/Lassen's Meadows for this 40-mile stretch of desert. A canteen or water keg is going to help a lot. Try to increase your pace of travel to 10 or even 12+ hours per day and to wait until sunset before crossing.

Truckee River

Once you reach the banks of the Truckee River, you've made it across the desert. This is a good place to stop and rest and change your pace back to normal. Before continuing, you have to decide how to cross the Truckee. It's often but not always shallow enough to ford. Be sure to check the current conditions first.

Truckee Canyons

The start of a very rugged stretch of trail.

Truckee Meadows/ Jameson's Station

A welcome stretch of green in dry country. In 1851 this became the site of another split in the trail, with the Beckwourth Cutoff heading northwest, and the main California Trail (the Truckee Route) going west-southwest. Most emigrants took the Truckee Route, though others swore by the Beckwourth Cutoff. A trading post known as Jameson's Station was established here in 1852, and was the first reliable source of supplies since French Ford Trading Post, more than 160 miles back.

Sierra Nevadas

A major mountain range and a big obstacle. Double-teaming usually gets you over the first long uphill climb (there are more later), though under less than ideal conditions ropes or chains may be necessary.

Truckee Lake/Donner Lake

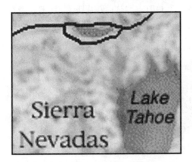

A large mountain lake that became one of the most famous landmarks in the history of the West, particularly after 1846. That was the year the famous Donner Party was stranded here after being caught in an unexpected autumn blizzard. To commemorate their ordeal, this lake's name was changed to Donner Lake in 1847. A year earlier, it became the site of a brief split in the trail, with the main route passing north of the lake (that was the route the Donner Party took) and the alternate road, known as the Cold Stream Pass Route, going south.

Rock Wall Ascent

Probably the single steepest, most difficult uphill climb on all the western trails. Using ropes or chains is the only practical way to get up this nearly vertical wall of stone. (Avoiding it was one of the reasons the Cold Stream Pass Route became popular.)

It's easy to get stuck when the weather or soil conditions are bad, and if you don't have ropes or chains, try to trade with somebody. Even with ropes or chains, your first try at the Rock Wall may fail. From 1846 on, you can always turn around and go back to the eastern edge of Truckee/Donner Lake, where you can take the Cold Stream Pass Route instead.

Truckee Pass/ Donner Pass

The beginning of a rough stretch of trail. After 1846 it was known as Donner Pass.

Summit Valley

Starting in 1846, this mountain valley is where the short Cold Stream Pass Route hooked back up with the main trail. Be sure to take the road to Johnson's Ranch; otherwise you're going in the wrong direction.

Johnson's Ranch

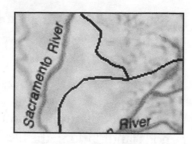

A supply point established in 1844. Emigrants would often stop to rest here following their ordeal in the Sierra Nevadas (which now lay behind). Beginning in 1851, this is where the Beckwourth Cutoff linked back up with the main trail. Make sure you take the road to Sutter's Fort.

American River

The American River posed the last big obstacle on the way to the Sacramento Valley. Sometimes it could be forded, but more often wagons had to caulk and float. In 1844 a ferry was established. It was followed in 1848 by a free bridge, which made the river no threat at all.

Sutter's Fort

Established in 1842, Sutter's Fort was a place to stock up on supplies before settling down in the Sacramento Valley. Starting in 1848, the Carson Route joined up with the main trail here. Be sure to take the road to Sacramento. Sutter's Fort was abandoned in 1852, though its crumbling buildings stood for years.

Sacramento Valley/ Sacramento

The end of the journey for wagons bound for California! The town of Sacramento was founded here in 1848.

The Salt Lake Cutoff

This was the primary route linking the Great Salt Lake Valley (later Great Salt Lake City) to the California Trail.

Weber River

This crossing of the Weber River is farther west than the one on the road from Blacks Fork Bend/Fort Bridger to the Great Salt Lake Valley. It's often but not always too deep to ford. A Mormon ferry was established here in 1847, offering the safest way across.

Bear River   Again, a more westerly crossing than the one near Blacks Fork Bend/Fort Bridger. Ferry service began in 1847.

Malad River   A toll bridge across this river was built in 1853. Before that, you had to ford or float.

Rattlesnake Pass   Not surprisingly, there are a lot of rattlesnakes around here. Watch out for snakebites!

Deep Creek   A relatively narrow stream but, as its name suggests, one that is usually much too deep to ford. No ferry or bridge was established here during the years of *Oregon Trail II*, so caulking and floating is almost always your best bet.

Raft River   The western trails crossed the Raft River in several places, but this wasn't one of them. On the Salt Lake Cutoff, wagon trains camped along the banks of the river for the water. A few miles west lies the Salt Lake Cutoff Junction, where the road links up with the California Trail. Unless you're headed for the Willamette Valley (Oregon City) in northern Oregon, be sure to choose the California Trail.

The Hastings Cutoff

Beginning in 1845, California-bound travelers could take this shortcut from the Great Salt Lake Valley. But the 70-mile desert crossing proved so difficult that few wagons chanced it. Still, it's an option if you're willing to take the risks. A word of warning: Don't take the Hastings Cutoff without a water keg or, at the very least, a canteen.

Utah Outlet/ Jordan River   A river that could sometimes be forded but more often required caulking and floating. In 1847 Mormon settlers established a ferry here and renamed it the Jordan River. A free bridge was built only a few years later, in 1850.

Tooele Valley
A fertile valley that gives you a chance to cut, gather, and store hay for your draft animals before the desert ahead. Don't pass this up.

Hastings Pass
The start of a rough stretch of trail.

Puddle Valley Knolls
A brief and easy descent into the Great Salt Lake Desert.

Great Salt Lake Desert
The most feared obstacle on all the western trails, this 70 mile wide, barren salt flat was utterly devoid of vegetation. The only water, aside from a very occasional shower or snow, was mixed in sticky mud that sometimes lay just beneath the salty soil—mud in which wagons easily got stuck.

When you reach the edge of the desert, be sure to pick up your pace to 12+ hours per day, and wait until sunset before crossing. Avoid stopping for any reason except dire emergencies. Even if you have a water keg and hay for your oxen (which are essential), they won't last forever. It can be a long, hard 70 miles.

Pilot Spring/ Donner Spring
A meager water spring signaling the end of the Great Salt Lake Desert. It's a good place to stop, rest, and slow your pace. It was renamed Donner Spring in 1847, as the Donner Party passed this way the year before.

Toano Range
An uphill climb through the mountains. Not especially difficult; double-teaming usually does the trick.

Pequop Mountains
Not much of a threat since you go around the mountains rather than over them.

Snow Water Lake A good source of water and an excellent place to stop and rest in this rough country.

Ruby Valley Marshes You have a pretty good chance of getting stuck in mud here. Beyond the marshes, the Hastings Cutoff goes through Overland Pass and then heads almost due north toward Emigrant Pass, where the road links with the California Trail.

The Hudspeth Cutoff

The Hudspeth Cutoff, which broke away from the Oregon Trail at Sheep Rock, bypassed Fort Hall, providing a shortcut to the California Trail. If you're confident that you have enough supplies to make it all the way to California (or, after 1849, at least as far as French Ford Trading Post) without restocking, this shortcut shaves several days off your journey.

Marsh Creek A rather narrow, shallow stream noted for the muddy trail leading to and from the crossing. Wagons can get stuck, especially if they're overloaded. A toll bridge was built here in 1852, and it's worth taking if you can afford it.

Raft River A more southerly crossing than the one on the main Oregon Trail. Caulking and floating is usually your best bet, though fording is possible when the water level is low. A short ways beyond the river lies the West End of the Hudspeth Cutoff, where you'll probably want to choose the California Trail option. But if you want to go to Oregon's Willamette Valley or if you're running low on supplies, take the road to Fort Hall.

The Carson Route

After it opened in 1848, the Carson Route was a popular choice to California's Sacramento Valley. It split off from the main trail at Humboldt Sink.

Forty Mile Desert

Regardless of whether you took the Truckee Route or the Carson Route, you still had to cross this desert. The standard desert precautions—have a canteen or water keg, gather hay beforehand, increase your pace of travel, and wait until nightfall before continuing—apply here.

Ragtown

This ramshackle collection of makeshift shacks and tents along the banks of the Carson River mark the end of the Forty Mile Desert for travelers on the Carson Route. It's a good place to stop, rest, and change your pace. A trading post was set up here in 1854, offering much-needed supplies.

Fort Churchill

This U.S. Army fort wasn't established until 1860, near the close of *Oregon Trail II*. If you're traveling then, it's a much better place to restock than the Ragtown trading post.

Virginia City

Founded in 1859, this boom town was the famed site of the Comstock silver strike. (You might recognize it as the town on the old *Bonanza* TV series.) Like all towns, it's an excellent place to buy supplies.

Eagle Ranch Trading Post/ Carson City

This supply point was established in 1851. Carson City, which later became the capital of Nevada, grew up around the trading post after 1858.

Mormon Station/Genoa

Another supply point, this one set up by Mormon entrepreneurs in 1849. The town of Genoa was founded in 1856.

Sierra Nevadas

The first encounter on the Carson Route of this great mountain range. But, unlike travelers on the Truckee and Beckwourth Routes, emigrants didn't strike directly across the Sierras. Instead, they traveled south along the foot of the mountains until they found a better entry point. So you don't need to make any major decisions yet.

West Carson River Canyon

Here you begin your uphill climb into and over the Sierra Nevadas. The canyon is long and rugged, but with a gradual rise in the path. Double-teaming should work.

Carson Pass

Once you've reached this rugged mountain pass, you're beyond the worst of the Sierras on the Carson Route.

Dry Diggins/ Hangtown/ Placerville

A rough frontier town near the western foot of the Sierra Nevadas. It's a good place to stop and rest after your mountain trek. The town's name was changed to Hangtown in 1850 and again to Placerville in mid-1854. Farther down the road, travelers on the Carson Route reached Sutter's Fort, where they connected with the main California Trail just east of Sacramento.

The Beckwourth Cutoff

The Beckwourth Cutoff, blazed by African-American mountain man James Beckwourth in 1851, splits off from the main California Trail at Truckee Meadows (later the site of Jameson's Station). It's a somewhat longer path than the Truckee Route, but many emigrants considered it less difficult.

Sierra Nevadas

As always, you have to cross the mountains. Double-teaming usually works, although ropes or chains make sense under bad conditions. This trail takes you through Beckwourth Pass, an alternate path through the Sierras discovered by James Beckwourth.

Beckwourth's Ranch

Beckwourth founded this supply point in 1851 and lived here for several years. He abandoned it in 1855, though the deteriorating buildings remained a landmark for many years.

Grizzly Ridge   The start of a steep downhill path out of the Sierras. It's a difficult descent, and ropes or chains may be necessary, especially when the trail is muddy or icy. If you don't have any ropes or chains, you may be able to trade for some.

Bidwell's Bar   A frontier town near the western foot of the mountains. It's a good place to rest and restock.

Marysville, California   Another frontier town, not to be confused with Marysville, Kansas. From here the Beckwourth Cutoff leads to Johnson's Ranch, where it joins the main California Trail (Truckee Route). You'll probably want the road to Sutter's Fort.

The Cold Stream Pass Route

The Cold Stream Pass Route was a very short stretch of trail offering another way around Truckee Lake (later Donner Lake).

Cold Stream Canyon   An uphill climb, but not as steep as the Rock Wall Ascent found on the main trail. Double-teaming will probably work.

Cold Stream Pass   The end of the uphill segment. A little ways on, the Cold Stream Pass Route joins the main trail at Summit Valley. Here you'll want to take the road to Johnson's Ranch.

The Applegate Route

Those who wanted to go to the Rogue River Valley of southern Oregon (the eventual site of the town of Jacksonville) broke off from the California Trail at the Applegate Cutoff, later called Lassen's Meadows. Remember there's a desert dead ahead, so if you're taking the Applegate Route, be sure to gather hay for your draft animals before moving on.

Black Rock Desert	Make the usual pre-desert preparations: Pick up your pace and wait until sunset before continuing.
Pahute Peak	A prominent landmark that signaled the end of the Black Rock Desert. While you can rest here, it might be better to wait until the next landmark, High Rock Creek, where there's a good source of water. But go ahead and slow your pace now.
High Rock Creek	A relatively narrow, shallow stream surrounded by steep rock walls that gave the creek its name. Fording usually works here, but check the current conditions.
Mountain Pass/Lassen's Pass/ Fandango Pass	A pass into the Warner Mountains. The name of this pass changed several times during the years of *Oregon Trail II*. Beginning in 1848 it was known as Lassen's Pass; in 1853 people started calling it Fandango Pass.
Warner Mountains	This range is a northern offshoot of the Sierra Nevadas. It's an uphill climb, but not quite so steep as the mountains farther south. Double-teaming usually works just fine.
Willow Creek Hill	The descent from the Warner Mountains toward Goose Lake. A relatively easy path, but take precautions, such as braking or anchoring.
Goose Lake	A good place to rest following your journey through the mountains. (Clear Lake and Lower Klamath Lake, a little farther down the trail, are also excellent spots.)
Klamath River	Usually not shallow enough to ford. A ferry was established here in 1852.
Siskiyou Mountains	Emigrants were anxious to get over these final mountains before the winter snows. Double-teaming will generally work under good conditions, but if the trail is snowy or icy, use ropes or chains and hope they work.

Emigrant Creek Hill   This mountain descent marks the last major obstacle on the Applegate Route. Use braking or anchoring.

Rogue River Valley/ Jacksonville   This fertile river valley marks the destination of most emigrants traveling the Applegate Route (some did continue north, but not in *Oregon Trail II*). In 1852 the town of Jacksonville was established, becoming the center of valley life for many decades.

A Complete List of Landmarks

The Main Oregon Trail

1   Independence (jumping-off town)
2   Blue River (free bridge 1859)
3   Westport
4   New Santa Fe
5   Blue Mound
6   Lawrence (founded 1854)
7   Topeka (founded 1854)
8   Kansas River
9   Saint Mary's Mission (founded 1848)
10   Red Vermillion River
11   Scott Spring
12   Alcove Spring
13   Big Blue River
14   St. Joseph Road Junction (established 1843)
15   Hollenberg Ranch (established 1857)
16   Rock Creek Station (established 1857)
17   The Narrows
18   Thirty-two Mile Station (established 1859)
19   "The Coast of Nebraska"
20   Fort Kearny (founded 1848)
21   Plum Creek
22   Midway Station (established 1859)
23   O'Fallon's Bluffs
24   South Platte River
25   California Hill
26   Windlass Hill
27   Ash Hollow

28   Courthouse and Jail Rocks

29   Chimney Rock

30   Scotts Bluff

31 a   Robidoux Pass (1840–47)

31 b   Robidoux Pass Trading Post (1848–52)

31 c   Mitchell Pass (1853–60)

32   Laramie River

33 a   Fort William (1840–41)

33 b   Fort John (rebuilt and renamed 1842; became
       trail junction 1847)

33 c   Fort Laramie (renamed 1849)

34   Register Cliff

35   Ayers Natural Bridge

36   North Platte River (free bridge 1859)

37   Mormon Ferry Trading Post
       (established mid-1847)

38   Emigrant Gap

39   Willow Springs

40   Independence Rock

41   Devil's Gate

42   Split Rock

43 a   Three Crossings (alternate route: #140)

43 b   Three Crossings Trading Post
       (established 1860; alternate route: #140)

44   Sweetwater River

45   Ice Spring Slough

46   Rocky Ridge

47 a   Lander Trading Post (established 1854)

47 b   Lander Cutoff
       (trail split 1858; alternate route: #143)

48   Final Sweetwater River Crossing

49   South Pass

50   Pacific Springs

51 a   Dry Sandy

51 b   Dry Sandy Trading Post (established 1859)

52   "Parting of the Ways"
       (established 1844; alternate route: #146)

53	Green River
54	Church Butte
55	Name Rock
56 a	Blacks Fork Bend (1840–41; alternate route: #148)
56 b	Fort Bridger (1842–Autumn 1857; alternate route: #148)
56 c	Fort Bridger Ruins (Autumn 1857– Spring 1858; alternate route: #148)
56 d	New Fort Bridger (Spring 1858–1860; alternate route: #148)
57	Grave Spring
58	West End of the Sublette Cutoff (established 1844)
59	Thomas Fork
60	Big Hill
61 a	Smith's Trading Post (established 1848)
61 b	Smith's Trading Post Ruins (post abandoned in 1851)
62	Soda Springs
63 a	Sheep Rock
63 b	Hudspeth Cutoff at Sheep Rock (established 1849; alternate route: #199)
64	West End of the Lander Cutoff (established 1858)
65	Fort Hall
66	Raft River
67	California Trail Junction (alternate route: #175)
68	Caldron Linn
69	Rock Creek Gorge
70	Rock Creek
71	Kanaka Rapids
72	Thousand Springs
73	Upper Salmon Falls

74   Three Islands
      (trail split; alternate route: #201)
75   Snake River
76   Hot Springs
77   Register Rock
78   Bonneville Point
79 a Fort Boise
79 b Fort Boise Ruins (fort abandoned in 1854)
80   Final Snake River Crossing
81   East Cow Hollow
82   Lytle Pass
83   Malheur River
84   Farewell Bend
85   Flagstaff Hill
86   Grande Ronde Valley
87   Grande Ronde River
88   Blue Mountains
89   Emigrant Hill
90   Doe Canyon (trail split 1840–54;
      alternate route: #206; no split 1855–60)
91 a Whitman Mission
91 b Whitman Mission Ruins
      (mission abandoned in late 1847)
92   Fort Walla Walla (abandoned in 1854 and
      thereafter inaccessible)
93   Trail Junction at the Umatilla River (1840–54)
94   Echo Meadows
95   Four Mile Canyon
96   McDonald Ford of the John Day River
97   Biggs Junction
98   Deschutes River
99   Deschutes Hill
100 a The Dalles (trail split 1846)
100 b Camp Drum at The Dalles (founded 1850)
100 c Camp Dalles (renamed 1853)
      (before 1846 go to #208; 1846–60:
      choice of #101 or #208)

The Barlow Toll Road (1846)

The Dalles/Camp Drum at The Dalles/Camp Dalles

101	Barlow Toll Road (established 1846)
102	Tygh Valley
103	Devil's Half Acre
104	Barlow Pass
105	Summit Meadows
106	Laurel Hill
107	Sandy River Toll Bridge
108 a	Willamette Valley (end of trail)
108 b	Oregon City (founded 1842; end of trail)

The St. Joseph Road (1843)

109	St. Joseph (jumping-off town founded 1843)
110	Missouri River
111	Cold Spring
112	Kennekuk Station (established 1858)
113	Walnut Creek (free bridge 1859)
114	Big Muddy Station (established 1859)
115	Vermillion River
116	Guittard's Station (established 1859)
117	Marysville, Kansas (founded 1851)
118	Big Blue River
	St. Joseph Road Junction (see #14)

The Mormon Trail (1846)

119	Nauvoo (jumping-off town beginning in 1846)
120	Mississippi River
121	Des Moines River
122	Garden Grove Waystation
123	Mount Pisgah Waystation (ceases operation in 1853)
124	Middle Nodaway River
125	Indian Town
126 a	Kanesville (founded 1846; jumping-off town beginning in 1847)
126 b	Council Bluffs (renamed 1854)
127	Kanesville Crossing of the Missouri River
128 a	Winter Quarters
128 b	Winter Quarters Ruins (settlement abandoned in late 1848)

128 c   Florence (founded 1854)
129   Elkhorn River
130   Pawnee Village
131   Loup River
132   Mormon Island
133   Deep Ravines
134   Sandy Bluffs
135   Cedar Bluffs
136   Castle Bluffs
137   Ancient Bluffs
138   Chimney Rock Vista
139   North Platte River
        Fort John/Fort Laramie (see #33b-c)

The Three Crossings Route

Three Crossings
140   First Sweetwater River Crossing
141   Second Sweetwater River Crossing
142   Third Sweetwater River Crossing
        Ice Spring Slough (see #45)

The Lander Cutoff (1858)

Lander Cutoff
143   Big Sandy Creek
144   New Fork River
145   Terrace Canyon
        West End of the Lander Cutoff (see #64)

The Sublette Cutoff (1844)

"Parting of the Ways"
146   Haystack Butte
147   Green River
        West End of the Sublette Cutoff (see #58)

The Salt Lake Alternate Route (later the western leg of the Mormon Trail)

Blacks Fork Bend/Fort Bridger
148   Bear River
149   The Needles
150   Echo Canyon
151   Weber River (free bridge 1858)
152   Pratt's Pass Canyon

153   Hogsback Summit

154   Dixie Hollow

155   East Canyon

156   Little Dutch Hollow

157   Big Mountain Pass

158   Big Mountain Descent

159   Little Mountain

160   Emigration Canyon Quarantine Station
       (established 1853)

161 a Steep Hill (climbed over until mid-1847)

161 b Donner Hill
       (renamed and circumvented after mid-1847)

162 a Great Salt Lake Valley
       (trail split 1845; alternate route: #211)

162 b Great Salt Lake City
       (founded mid-1847; optional end of trail)

The Hastings   *Great Salt Lake Valley/Great Salt Lake City*
Cutoff (1845)
163 a Utah Outlet (1845–46)

163 b Jordan River
       (renamed 1847; free bridge 1850)

164   South Shore of the Great Salt Lake

165   Tooele Valley

166   Skull Valley

167   Hastings Pass

168   Puddle Valley Knolls

169   Great Salt Lake Desert

170 a Pilot Spring

170 b Donner Spring (renamed 1847)

171   Toano Range

172   Pequop Mountains

173   Snow Water Lake

174   Ruby Valley Marshes
       Emigrant Pass (see #181)

**The Main
California
Trail
(including the
Truckee
Route)**

California Trail Junction

175   West End of the Hudspeth Cutoff
          (established 1849)

176   City of Rocks

177   Salt Lake Cutoff Junction

178   Granite Mountain

179   Granite Mountain Pass

180 a   North Fork of Mary's River

180 b   North Fork of the Humboldt River
          (renamed 1845)

181   Emigrant Pass (trail junction 1845)

182 a   Gravelly Ford of Mary's River

182 b   Gravelly Ford of the Humboldt River
          (renamed 1845)

183   French Ford Trading Post (established 1850)

184 a   Applegate Cutoff
          (trail split 1846; alternate route: #216)

184 b   Lassen's Meadows (renamed 1848)

185   Big Meadows

186 a   Mary's Sink

186 b   Humboldt Sink (renamed 1845;
          trail split 1848; alternate route: #230)

187   Forty Mile Desert

188   Truckee River

189 a   Truckee Meadows
          (trail split 1851; alternate route: #240)

189 b   Jameson's Station at Truckee Meadows
          (established 1852)

190   Sierra Nevadas

191 a   Truckee Lake
          (trail split 1846; alternate route: #245)

191 b   Donner Lake (renamed 1847)

192   Rock Wall Ascent

193 a   Truckee Pass

193 b   Donner Pass (renamed 1847)

194   Summit Valley (trail junction 1846)

195   Johnson's Ranch
       (established 1844; trail junction 1851)
196   American River (free bridge 1848)
197 a Sutter's Fort
       (founded 1842; trail junction 1848)
197 b Sutter's Fort Ruins (fort abandoned in 1852)
198 a Sacramento Valley (end of trail)
198 b Sacramento (founded 1848; end of trail)

The Hudspeth Cutoff (1849)

Hudspeth Cutoff at Sheep Rock
199   Marsh Creek
200   Raft River
       West End of the Hudspeth Cutoff (see #175)

The South Alternate Route

Three Islands
201   Bruneau Sand Dunes
202   Bruneau River
203   Castle Butte
204   Sinker Creek Butte
205   Givens Hot Springs
       East Cow Hollow (see #81)

The Umatilla Shortcut

Doe Canyon
206   Umatilla Valley
207   Umatilla River
       Trail Junction at the Umatilla River (see #93; does not appear from 1855 on; see #94)

Rafting Down the Columbia

The Dalles/Camp Drum at The Dalles/Camp Dalles
208   Cascades Portage
209   McCord Creek
210   Fort Vancouver
       Willamette Valley/Oregon City (see #108a-b)

The Salt Lake Cutoff

Great Salt Lake Valley/Great Salt Lake City
211   Weber River
212   Bear River
213   Malad River
214   Rattlesnake Pass

215   Deep Creek
       Salt Lake Cutoff Junction (see #177)

**The Applegate
Road (1846)**

Applegate Cutoff/Lassen's Meadows
216   Black Rock Desert
217   Pahute Peak
218   High Rock Creek
219   Middle Alkali Lake
220 a Mountain Pass
220 b Lassen's Pass (renamed 1848)
220 c Fandango Pass (renamed 1853)
221   Warner Mountains
222   Willow Creek Hill
223   Goose Lake
224   Clear Lake
225   Lower Klamath Lake
226   Klamath River
227   Siskiyou Mountains
228   Emigrant Creek Hill
229 a Rogue River Valley (end of trail)
229 b Jacksonville (founded 1852; end of trail)

**The Carson
Route (1848)**

Humboldt Sink
230   Forty Mile Desert
231   Ragtown (trading post added in 1854)
232   Fort Churchill (founded 1860)
233   Virginia City (founded 1859)
234 a Eagle Ranch Trading Post (established 1851)
234 b Carson City (founded 1853)
235 a Mormon Station (established 1849)
235 b Genoa (founded 1856)
236   Sierra Nevadas
237   West Carson River Canyon
238   Carson Pass
239 a Dry Diggins
239 b Hangtown (renamed 1850)
239 c Placerville (renamed Spring 1854)
       Sutter's Fort (see #197a-b)

The Beckwourth Cutoff (1851)

Truckee Meadows/Jameson's Station

240   Sierra Nevadas
241 a   Beckwourth's Ranch
241 b   Beckwourth's Ranch Ruins
         (ranch abandoned in 1852)
242   Grizzly Ridge
243   Bidwell's Bar
244   Marysville, California
         Johnson's Ranch (see #195)

The Cold Stream Pass Route (1846)

Truckee Lake/Donner Lake

245   Cold Stream Canyon
246   Cold Stream Pass
         Summit Valley (see #194)

TRAIL MAPS IN OREGON TRAIL II

The detailed trail maps on the following pages appear in *Oregon Trail II*. The map below gives an overview of the area these maps cover.

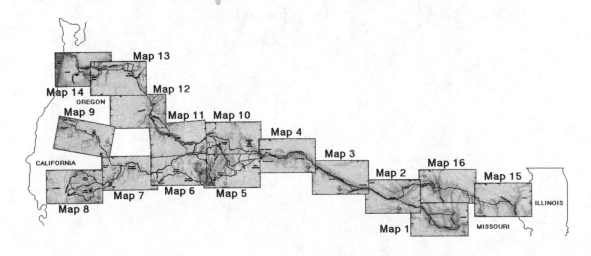

Map 1: The First Leg of the Oregon Trail

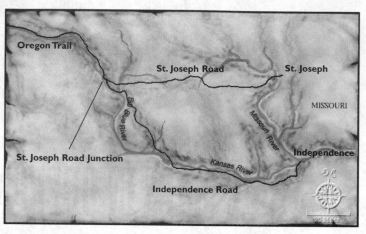

At the St. Joseph Road Junction (1843–on):

⚙ If you want to head west to any of the trail destinations, take the Oregon Trail heading west.

⚙ If you want to go to Independence, Missouri, take the Independence Road.

⚙ If you want to go to St. Joseph, Missouri, take the St. Joseph Road.

CHAPTER 13

Map 2: Along the Platte River

There are no splits along this part of the trail.

Map 3: Near Chimney Rock

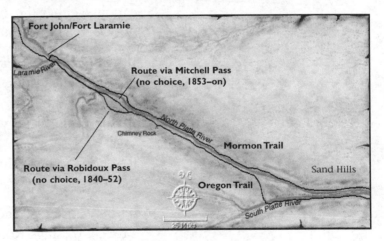

At Fort John/Fort Laramie (1847–on):

- ✳ If you want to continue west toward any of the trail destinations, take the Oregon Trail heading west.

- ✳ If you want to go back east, take either the Mormon Trail or the Platte River Road heading east.

Map 4: Near Independence Rock

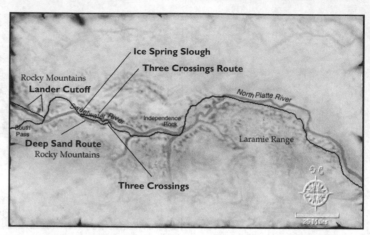

At Three Crossings (all years):

⚙ If you want to continue west on the trail, you can take either the Three Crossings Route or the Deep Sand Route.

⚙ If you want to go back east, take the road to Independence Rock.

At Ice Spring Slough (all years):

⚙ If you want to continue west on the trail, take the road to South Pass.

⚙ If you want to go back east, take either the Three Crossings Route or the Deep Sand Route.

At Lander Cutoff (1858–on):

✳ If you want to take a shortcut to Fort Hall, take the Lander Cutoff.

✳ If you want to go to Fort Bridger, take the road to South Pass.

✳ If you want to go back east toward one of the jumping-off towns, take the road to Independence Rock.

Map 5: Near Blacks Fork Bend/ Fort Bridger

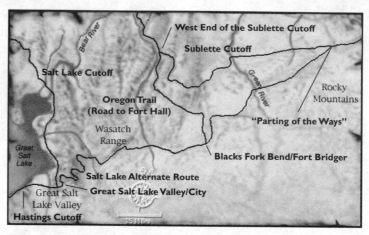

At "Parting of the Ways" (1844–on):

✳ If you want to go to Fort Bridger or the Great Salt Lake Valley, take the road to Fort Bridger.

✳ If you want to take a shortcut to Fort Hall, take the Sublette Cutoff.

✳ If you want to head back east, take the road to South Pass.

At Blacks Fork Bend/Fort Bridger (all years):

✳ If you want to go to Fort Hall or the Willamette Valley, take the road to Fort Hall.

✳ If you want to go to the Great Salt Lake Valley, take the Salt Lake Alternate Route.

✳ If you want to head back east, take the road to South Pass.

At the West End of the Sublette Cutoff (1844–on):

- If you want to go to Fort Hall or the Willamette Valley, take the road to Fort Hall.

- If you want to go to Fort Bridger or the Great Salt Lake Valley, take the road to Fort Bridger.

- If you want to head back east, take the Sublette Cutoff.

At Great Salt Lake Valley/Great Salt Lake City (1845–on):

- If you want to go to the Willamette Valley or take the standard route to California or the Rogue River Valley, take the Salt Lake Cutoff.

- If you want to take a shortcut to California or the Rogue River Valley via the Great Salt Lake Desert, take the Hastings Cutoff.

- If you want to head back east, take the road to Fort Bridger.

Map 6: Near the Great Salt Lake Desert

At the Salt Lake Cutoff Junction (all years):

⚙ If you want to go to California or the Rogue River Valley, take the California Trail.

⚙ If you want to go to Fort Hall or the Willamette Valley, take the road to Fort Hall.

⚙ If you want to go to the Great Salt Lake Valley, take the Salt Lake Cutoff.

At Emigrant Pass (1845–on):

⚙ If you want to go to California or the Rogue River Valley, take the California Trail.

⚙ If you want to go to Fort Hall or the Willamette Valley, take the road to Fort Hall.

⚙ If you want to go to the Great Salt Lake Valley via the Great Salt Lake Desert, take the Hastings Cutoff.

Map 7: Along the Humboldt River

At Applegate Cutoff/Lassen's Meadows (1846–on):

- ✸ If you want to go to the Sacramento Valley, take the California Trail.

- ✸ If you want to go to the Rogue River Valley in southern Oregon, take the Applegate Road.

- ✸ If you want to head back east, take the road to Emigrant Pass.

At Humboldt Sink (1848–on):

- ✸ If you want to take the newer, more southerly road into California, take the Carson Route.

- ✸ If you want to take the older, more northerly road into California, take the Truckee Route.

- ✸ If you want to go anywhere other than California, take the road to Emigrant Pass.

Map 8: Approaches to the Sacramento Valley

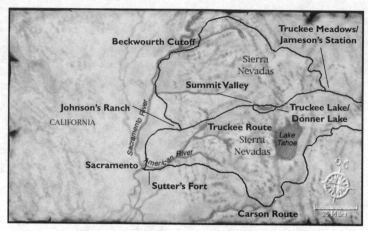

At Truckee Meadows/Jameson's Station (1851–on):

⊛ If you want to take the northern route to the Sacramento Valley, take the Beckwourth Cutoff.

⊛ If you want to take the central route to the Sacramento Valley, take the Truckee Route.

⊛ If you want to go anywhere else, take the road to Emigrant Pass.

At Truckee Lake/Donner Lake (1846–on):

⊛ If you want to go to the Sacramento Valley via the trail that passes south of Truckee/Donner Lake, take the Cold Stream Pass Route.

⊛ If you want to go to Sacramento via the trail that passes north of the lake, take the Truckee Route.

⊛ If you want to go anywhere else, take the road to Truckee Meadows.

At Summit Valley (1846–on):

✳ If you want to go to the Sacramento Valley, take the road to Johnson's Ranch.

✳ If you want to go anywhere else, take either the Cold Stream Pass Route or the main road to Truckee Meadows.

At Johnson's Ranch (1851–on):

✳ If you want to go to the Sacramento Valley, take the road to Sutter's Fort.

✳ If you want to go anywhere else, take either the Beckwourth Cutoff or the main road to Truckee Meadows.

At Sutter's Fort (1848–on):

✳ If you want to enter the Sacramento Valley, take the road to Sacramento.

✳ If you want to go anywhere else, take either the Carson Route or the Truckee Route.

Map 9: The Trail into the Rogue River Valley

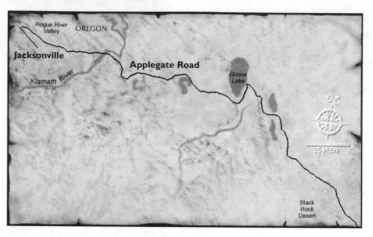

There are no splits along this part of the trail.

Map 10: Near Soda Springs

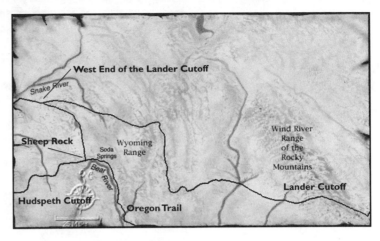

At Sheep Rock (1849–on):

⊛   If you want to bypass Fort Hall on the way to California or the Rogue River Valley, take the Hudspeth Cutoff.

⊛   If you want to go to Fort Hall or if you're going to the Willamette Valley, take the road to Fort Hall.

⊛   If you want to go to Great Salt Lake City or head back east, take the road to Fort Bridger.

At the West End of the Lander Cutoff (1858–on):

⊛   If you want to go to Fort Hall, California, the Rogue River Valley, or the Willamette Valley, take the road to Fort Hall.

⊛   If you want to go to Great Salt Lake City, take the road to Fort Bridger.

⊛   If you want to head back east, take the Lander Cutoff.

Map 11: Near Three Islands

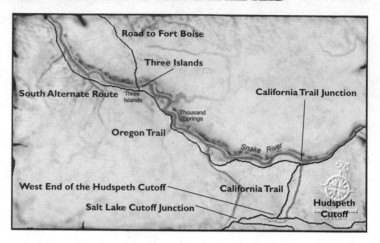

At the California Trail Junction (all years):

✳ If you want to go to California, the Great Salt Lake Valley, or the Rogue River Valley, take the California Trail.

✳ If you want to go to the Willamette Valley, take the Oregon Trail.

✳ If you want to go back east, take the road to Fort Hall.

At Three Islands (all years):

✳ If you want to bypass Fort Boise and avoid crossing the Snake River on the way to the Willamette Valley, take the South Alternate Route.

✳ If you want to go to Fort Boise on the way to the Willamette Valley, take the road to Fort Boise.

✳ If you want to go anywhere else or head back east, take the road to Fort Hall.

At the West End of the Hudspeth Cutoff (1849–on):

✳ If you want to go to California, the Rogue River Valley, or Great Salt Lake City, take the California Trail.

✳ If you want to go to Fort Hall or the Willamette Valley, take the road to Fort Hall.

✳ If you want to head back east, take the Hudspeth Cutoff.

At the Salt Lake Cutoff Junction (all years):

✳ If you want to go to California or the Rogue River Valley, take the California Trail.

✳ If you want to go to Fort Hall or the Willamette Valley, take the road to Fort Hall.

✳ If you want to go to the Great Salt Lake Valley, take the Salt Lake Cutoff.

Map 12: Near Farewell Bend

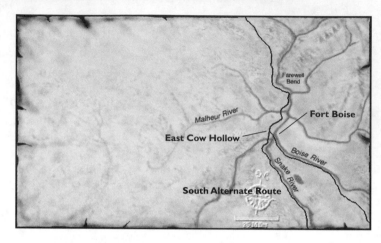

At East Cow Hollow (all years):

⊛   If you want to go to the Willamette Valley, take the road to Farewell Bend.

⊛   If you're low on supplies and need to reach a fort as soon as possible, take the road to Fort Boise.

⊛   If you want to head back east, take the South Alternate Route.

Map 13: Near the Blue Mountains

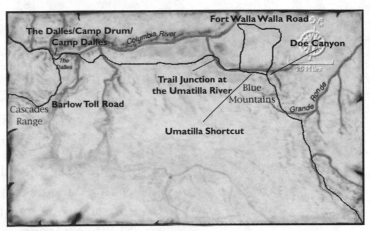

At Doe Canyon (1840–1854):

✳ If you want to go to Fort Walla Walla and/or the Whitman Mission on the way to the Willamette Valley, take the Fort Walla Walla Road.

✳ If you want to bypass Fort Walla Walla and the Whitman Mission, take the Umatilla Shortcut.

✳ If you want to head back east, take the road that goes back up Emigrant Hill.

At the Trail Junction at the Umatilla River (1840–1854):

✳ If you want to go to the Willamette Valley, take the road to The Dalles.

✳ If you want to go to Fort Walla Walla and/or the Whitman Mission, take the Fort Walla Walla Road.

✳ If you want to head back east, take the Umatilla Shortcut.

At The Dalles, later called Camp Drum or Camp Dalles (1846–on):

✳ If you want to follow the land route to the Willamette Valley, take the Barlow Toll Road.

✳ If you want to raft down the Columbia River to the Willamette Valley and are willing to do your own rafting, choose the option to raft down the Columbia.

✳ If you want to go down the Columbia River to the Willamette Valley and are willing to hire someone to raft you, choose the option to hire someone to raft you.

Map 14: Approaches to the Willamette Valley

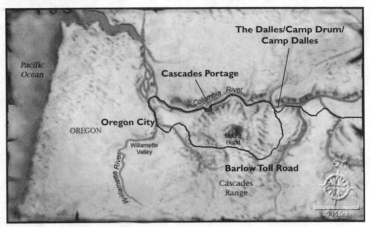

At The Dalles (1846–on):

⚙ If you want to follow the land route to the Willamette Valley, take the Barlow Toll Road.

⚙ If you want to raft down the Columbia River to the Willamette Valley and are willing to do your own rafting, choose the option to raft down the Columbia.

⚙ If you want to go down the Columbia River to the Willamette Valley and are willing to hire someone to raft you, choose the option to hire someone to raft you.

At Cascades Portage (all years):

⚙ If you want to take the land route around the rapids, choose the option to portage around the rapids.

⚙ If you want to risk going through the rapids (not recommended), choose the option to continue through the rapids.

Map 15: The First Leg of the Mormon Trail

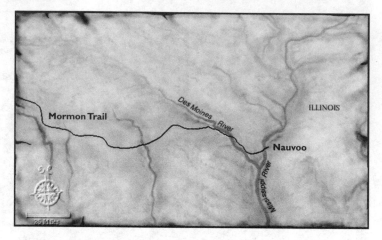

There are no splits along this stretch of the trail.

Map 16: Near Kanesville/ Council Bluffs

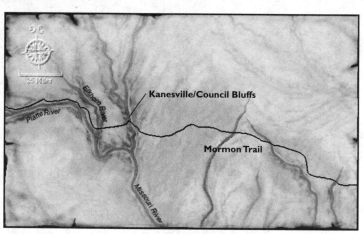

There are no splits along this stretch of the trail.

HISTORICAL CHARACTERS IN OREGON TRAIL II

In *Oregon Trail II* you meet nearly 200 speaking characters. Most of them only represent the types of people you might have encountered on the western trails. Some of them, however, are true historical figures who lived at the time and place you find them.

The historical characters in *Oregon Trail II* are listed below in alphabetical order.

James (Jim) Beckwourth (1798-1866)

An African-American trapper, trader, scout, and frontier businessman, Beckwourth was born in Virginia as the son of an enslaved mother and a white slave owner. He received some schooling and was freed by his father, after which he moved west.

For a time he worked as a blacksmith in St. Louis, but soon his lifelong restlessness got the better of him, and he moved on. For several years he lived among the Crow Indians, gaining notoriety as a warrior and even

Jim Beckwourth
as portrayed by
Lawrence Peterson

becoming a chief. He fought with the U.S. forces in the Mexican War, was a scout for John C. Frémont, and discovered Beckwourth Pass through the Sierra Nevadas in 1850.

The following year he blazed a path to California through that pass, building a ranch where travelers could stop. Beckwourth lived at this ranch for several years, but abandoned it in 1855. In *Oregon Trail II*, you may meet him at Beckwourth's Ranch from 1851 through 1854.

James (Jim) Bridger (1804-1881)

One of the best-known mountain men of the West, Bridger was a famous fur trader, scout, and explorer. He was born in Richmond, Virginia, and in 1822, at age 18, joined a fur-trapping expedition heading west.

The following year, he was a member of the first American trapping expedition to journey west of the Rocky Mountains, and continued exploring the west on foot for the next twenty years.

He's believed to be the first non-Hispanic, white American to lay eyes on the Great Salt Lake, which he first visited in 1824. In 1843, along with his trading partner Louis Vasquez, he established Fort Bridger, which quickly became a major supply point for trappers, traders, and pioneers.

Jim Bridger
as portrayed by
James L. Thompson

In 1855 Bridger sold his fort to the Mormons and later served as a scout and guide on various expeditions, including some for the U.S. Army.

In *Oregon Trail II*, you may meet him at Fort Bridger between 1843 and 1855. There's a good chance you'll see him at other locations, too, as you travel through the western territories.

**Dr. John
McLoughlin
(1784-1857)**

Dr. John McLoughlin
*as portrayed by
Dale LaFrenz*

For more than two decades, Dr. John McLoughlin ran Fort Vancouver, which he established in 1825 as a fur-trading post for the Hudson's Bay Company. A British subject born in Quebec, Canada, and the chief officer of a British outpost, he nevertheless welcomed Americans. He often helped them settle in Oregon Country by letting them purchase supplies on credit. He also dealt fairly with the local Indians, who called him "Great White Eagle" because of his long gray hair.

After the United States took over the southern half of the Oregon Country in 1846, Fort Vancouver became an army installation, and McLoughlin resigned. He moved a few miles south to the growing settlement of Oregon City, which he'd founded several years before, and became a U.S. citizen.

McLoughlin lived in Oregon City for the rest of his life and was honored, then as now, as "The Father of Oregon." You may see him if you visit Fort Vancouver before 1846.

**Joseph
Pappan**

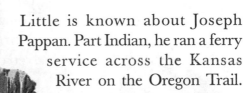

Joseph Pappan
*as portrayed by
Tom Naughton*

Little is known about Joseph Pappan. Part Indian, he ran a ferry service across the Kansas River on the Oregon Trail. Along with his brother Louis, Joseph Pappan (sometimes spelled Papin) ran the ferry beginning in 1844.

You may get a chance to meet him if you reach the Kansas River crossing from 1844 on. By the way, there happens to be another fellow traveling about in *Oregon Trail II* who bears a striking resemblance to Mr. Pappan, but it's not him.

Thomas "Peg-Leg" Smith

Thomas "Peg-Leg" Smith
as depicted in a digital composite

Another historical figure about whom little is known, Smith was a mountain man who established a trading post along the Oregon Trail near the Bear River in 1848. He abandoned the post less than three years later.

He was nicknamed "Peg-Leg" after a serious accident that required him to amputate his own leg. You'll probably meet him if you arrive at Smith's Trading Post between 1848 and 1851.

Johann (John) Sutter (1803-1880)

Johann Sutter
as depicted in a digital composite

Born in Germany but a resident of Switzerland, Sutter came to California in 1839. He persuaded the local Mexican officials (California was part of Mexico at the time) to give him a land grant near the junction of the Sacramento and American Rivers, where he established a trading fort in 1842. Sutter's Fort became the center of a growing settlement, which Sutter called "New Helvetia" (Latin for Switzerland).

In 1846, during the Mexican War, the U.S. Army temporarily took control of the fort. Sutter owned extensive land holdings in central California, but his claims were sometimes tenuous. Gold was discovered on his lands in 1848, but instead of bringing him fortune, it brought financial ruin as thousands of squatters overran his land and even his own employees abandoned their work to search for gold. U.S. courts later rejected his Mexican land grants.

By 1852 he was bankrupt, so he moved east, abandoning Sutter's Fort. He spent the rest of his life unsuccessfully lobbying Congress to redress his misfortune. You may meet him at Sutter's Fort between 1842 and 1852.

Louis Vieux

Louis Vieux
as portrayed by
Rich Bergeron

Not much is known about Louis Vieux except that he was a part-French chief of the Potawatomi Indians. He built a toll bridge across the Red Vermillion River in 1848. It quickly became the favored means for wagons to cross the sometimes treacherous river. Vieux charged one dollar per wagon, and it's thought that during the peak years of westward migration he took in roughly $300 per day. This made him a wealthy man.

Vieux also sold and traded goods to emigrants. You may meet him if you arrive at the Red Vermillion River from 1848 on.

Washakie (c. 1804-1900)

Washakie
as depicted in a
digital composite

A chief of the Wind River Shoshoni, who lived in what is now southwestern Wyoming, Washakie was friendly with Americans and often assisted pioneers. Living near the Green River crossing on the trail to Fort Bridger, he and his people traded with emigrants and helped them cross the river.

He's one of the few Native Americans to have a U.S. Army fort named after him—Fort Washakie in Wyoming—and when he died, he was buried with full military honors. You may meet him at the southernmost Green River crossing just about any year, although he probably won't be there during the winter.

Dr. Marcus Whitman (1802-1847)

Dr. Marcus Whitman
*as depicted in a
digital composite*

A physician and Methodist missionary who settled in the Oregon Country in 1835, Whitman established a mission among the Cayuse Indians near modern-day Walla Walla, Washington. He returned east in 1842 to raise money for his mission and recruit new settlers. The following year he led more than 900 people back to Oregon, the largest wagon train west up to that time.

The Whitman Mission was an important stop on the Oregon Trail, where needy pioneers sought supplies and medical help. But it was abandoned after an Indian attack on November 29, 1847. A group of Cayuse warriors, fearful and angry over a deadly measles epidemic they blamed on the settlers, fought and killed most of the mission's inhabitants, including Dr. Whitman and his wife.

Narcissa Whitman (d. 1847)

Narcissa Whitman
*as portrayed by
Michelle LeMay*

The wife of Dr. Marcus Whitman and, like him, a Methodist missionary among the Cayuse Indians in the Oregon Country. In 1835 she became one of the first two European-American women to cross the continent of North America over the Oregon Trail. Her daughter Alice (who later drowned in an accident) was the first white American child born in the Oregon Country. Narcissa Whitman was killed along with her husband when Indians attacked their mission. You may meet both Whitmans at their mission before November 29, 1847.

Other Historical Figures

A number of other historical figures are mentioned in conversations in *Oregon Trail II*, including Christopher "Kit" Carson, John C. Frémont, Francis Parkman, Frederick Lander, and Samuel Barlow. A great many other historical names are seen in newspaper headlines in the jumping-off towns and other towns along the way.

CHRONOLOGY 1840 – 1860

The following is a chronological list of historical events relevant to the Oregon, California, and Mormon Trails. Events in boldface have direct consequences for you. Other events listed are reflected in more subtle ways in *Oregon Trail II*. For instance, characters may talk about these events, but nothing more. Specific dates are noted when available.

1840-1841

Estimated traffic on trails between 1840 and 1841: 200 emigrants.

The first large wagon train (48 wagons) sets out for the Sacramento Valley.

Brigham Young travels to England to talk about the Mormon Church (the Church of Jesus Christ of Latter-Day Saints). As a direct result, thousands of English converts go to Nauvoo, Illinois, to join the growing Mormon settlement there.

Sutter's Fort is established in 1841, near the junction of the Sacramento and American Rivers, by Swiss immigrant Johann Sutter.

Adobe buildings improve Fort William. (Previously all buildings were made of logs.)

The Bidwell-Bartleson party leaves Westport, Missouri, in 1841, led by mountain man Thomas Fitzpatrick. The party splits after South Pass, one group going on to Oregon and the other (led by Bidwell) heading for California. Late in the journey, John Bidwell leads the first large wagon train across the Sierra Nevadas.

1842

Estimated traffic on trails in 1842: 200.

May 15   Dr. Elijah White sets off from Independence, Missouri, leading a party of 130 people and 18 wagons, heading for the Whitman Mission. Lansford Hastings, a lawyer from Ohio, travels with the White party.

May 22   John C. Frémont sets off from St. Louis on an expedition exploring the eastern half of the Oregon Trail, up to the Rocky Mountains. Kit Carson serves as his guide.

June 20   The Frémont party camps on the western bank of the Big Blue River.

June 22   The Frémont party "noons" at what will later become the site of Rock Creek Station.

August 8   Frémont reaches South Pass.

October 3   Dr. Marcus Whitman leaves the Oregon Country for Boston and Washington, D.C., to encourage missionary work and emigration to Oregon.

Other Events of 1842

Lansford Hastings, who traveled to Oregon with the White party, dislikes the Oregon Country and moves to California.

Fort William's name is changed to Fort John, but people call it Fort Laramie after the Laramie River.

Fort Bridger is established by mountain man Jim Bridger and his business partner, Louis Vasquez.

Oregon City is founded by Dr. John McLoughlin, the British administrator of Fort Vancouver.

1843

Estimated traffic on trails in 1843: 1,000.

Early May   Frémont sets out from Missouri on his second expedition.

May 2   Settlers in the Oregon Country hold a meeting in Champoeg to organize a territorial government.

May 22   The "Great Migration" begins with more than a thousand people leaving Independence, Missouri, in wagon trains. Marcus Whitman, on his return trip to Oregon, travels with them.

July 5   Oregon settlers adopt a preliminary territorial constitution modeled on the laws of Iowa, but the U.S. does not yet have full jurisdiction there.

July 26   Dr. Whitman's wagon train rests at Independence Rock.

September 9   Frémont explores the southern shores of the Great Salt Lake.

October 3   Frémont is at Three Island Crossing.

October 16   The first wagons of the "Great Migration" reach Fort Walla Walla.

October 27   The first wagons of the "Great Migration" reach Oregon City.

Other Events of 1843

The first reasonably accurate map of the Oregon Trail, prepared by cartographer Charles Preuss and based on information from the Frémont expedition, is published. Frémont's accompanying narrative serves as a guidebook for later emigrants.

Joseph Robidoux founds the town of St. Joseph, Missouri, which soon rivals Independence as a popular jumping-off town.

Jim Bridger and Louis Vasquez build a new Fort Bridger near the old one.

1844

Estimated traffic on trails in 1844: 2,000.

February   Frémont is in the Sierra Nevadas, facing the hardships of a winter mountain crossing.

March   Frémont arrives at Sutter's Fort.

March 22 through June 1   **A period of unusually heavy, almost constant rain in Kansas and eastern Nebraska, so much so that rivers are swollen and nearly impassable. Most low-lying regions are flooded. During this period of more than two months there are reportedly only eight days without rain.**

June 27   Mormon leader Joseph Smith is killed by a mob near Nauvoo, Illinois. Brigham Young becomes the new Mormon leader.

July   Frémont returns to Missouri from his second expedition.

| November | Some traders build a cabin near what will later be known as Donner Lake. Two years later some members of the Donner Party (the Breen family) will use this cabin. |

Other Events of 1844

Ferry service across the Kansas River begins, run by the Pappan brothers, Joseph and Louis.

The Sublette Cutoff is established.

African-American pioneer George Washington Bush crosses the plains to Oregon with a wagon train. He earned a fortune trading cattle in Missouri, but moves to Oregon to escape hostility toward free blacks. Bush, his wife, and five children are the first American settlers near Puget Sound.

Elisha Stevens successfully captains a wagon train to California.

Lansford Hastings returns east from California and writes his famous *The Emigrants' Guide to Oregon and California,* published the following year (1845).

The Oregon Country, control of which is still shared with Great Britain, becomes a major issue in the U.S. presidential campaign. "Fifty-four Forty or Fight!" and "All of Oregon or None!" are popular slogans in Democrat James K. Polk's campaign. He wins the election.

1845

Estimated traffic on trails in 1845: 5,000.

| Early May | Frémont starts his third western expedition, again with Carson. |
| October 18 | Frémont once again explores the shores of the Great Salt Lake. |

Other Events of 1845

Lansford Hastings establishes the Hastings Cutoff.

Oregon City is named capital of the provisional Oregon Territory. It remains the capital until 1851.

Col. Stephen Watts Kearny leads the first large military expedition up the Platte River along the Oregon Trail. He holds an Indian *powwow* at Fort John.

Stephen Meek's party strays from the Oregon Trail after crossing the Malheur River and meets with disaster. The survivors finally reach The Dalles.

Samuel K. Barlow begins work on his toll road, which will open the following year.

Frémont renames Mary's River the Humboldt River.

1846

Estimated traffic on trails in 1846: 1,000.

January	Frémont is once again in California.
April	**The great Mormon trek begins from Nauvoo, Illinois.**
April	Francis Parkman sets out on the Oregon Trail.
May	The Donner Party sets out from Independence, Missouri.
May 13	The Mexican War begins with the U.S. declaration of war.
May 29	The Donner Party camps at Alcove Spring.
June 3	Col. Kearny occupies Santa Fe and moves from there to California.
June 14	American settlers proclaim the Republic of California.
June 15	The U.S. and Britain sign a treaty agreeing to divide the Oregon Country along the 49th parallel.
July 4	The Donner Party reaches Fort John.
July 5	Frémont assumes control of U.S. forces in California.

July 28–30	The Donner Party rests at Fort Bridger.
August 17	Commodore David Stockton declares that California has been annexed by the United States.
September	Francis Parkman returns to Westport, Missouri. His travels later become the basis of his book *The Oregon Trail*.
September 4	The Donner Party camps on the southern shore of the Great Salt Lake.
October 28	**An early blizzard in the Sierra Nevadas traps the Donner Party. It snows heavily for several days. Later, the Donner Party makes winter camp along the shores of Truckee Lake. The same early snows that trap the Donner Party also wreak havoc in the northern Sierras, where emigrants traveling the Applegate Road are snowed in. Many perish.**
November 5	Stockton and Frémont are ordered to turn command and control of California over to Kearny.
December 28	Iowa becomes a state.

Other Events of 1846

Mormon pioneers establish Winter Quarters.

The British turn control of Fort Vancouver over to the United States. Chief Factor Dr. John McLoughlin (who has always helped U.S. settlers) retires, settles in Oregon City, and later becomes a U.S. citizen.

The Barlow Toll Road opens, creating a land route for the final leg of the journey to the Willamette Valley.

1847

Estimated traffic on trails in 1847: 2,000.

January 10–13	Remaining Mexican forces in California surrender to Kearny (now promoted to General) and Frémont.

January 16	Stockton, refusing to recognize Kearny's authority, appoints Frémont governor of California.
March through April	Survivors of the Donner Party reach Sutter's Fort.
April 16	Brigham Young leads a small party of Mormons westward from Winter Quarters.
May 31	Kearny appoints Richard B. Mason governor of California. He heads for Washington, D.C., with Stockton and Frémont, to resolve their conflict.
July 4	An emigrant party hauls a cannon to the top of Independence Rock and fires it in celebration of Independence Day.
July 24	**Mormons reach the valley of the Great Salt Lake and establish Great Salt Lake City and the "State of Deseret."**
November 29	**The "Whitman Massacre": Whitman Mission is attacked by Cayuse Indians (led by Chief Tilokaikt) who blame the Whitmans for a severe measles epidemic destroying their village. The Whitmans and other settlers are killed and the mission abandoned. This starts the "Cayuse War," which rages until 1850.**

Other Events of 1847

Truckee Pass and Truckee Lake are renamed Donner Pass and Donner Lake for the Donner Party. Other western landmarks are also renamed in commemoration.

Mormons begin ferry service across the North Platte, Green, Bear, and Weber Rivers.

The Mormon Ferry Trading Post is established.

The Applegate Road to southern Oregon is opened.

Daniel Lee's Methodist Mission at The Dalles (founded in 1838) is abandoned in the wake of the "Whitman Massacre."

1848

Estimated traffic on trails in 1848: 4,000.

January 24   While building a sawmill for Johann Sutter along the American River, James W. Marshall discovers gold 40 miles east of Sutter's Fort.

February 2   The Treaty of Guadalupe Hidalgo ends the Mexican War. U.S. sovereignty over Texas is recognized and the United States formally annexes California, Nevada, Utah, and parts of Wyoming, Colorado, New Mexico, and Arizona.

May   Locust swarms almost destroy Mormon crops near Great Salt Lake City but are devoured by seagulls.

August 14   The Oregon Territory is formally organized with Gen. Joseph Lane serving as first governor.

August 19   New York newspapers report the discovery of gold in California, confirmed by the U.S. government several months later.

Other Events of 1848

A U.S. army stockade is built at The Dalles.

Mormons establish a ferry across the Elkhorn River.

St. Mary's Mission is founded by Jesuit missionaries.

Robidoux Pass Trading Post is established.

A toll bridge is built across the Red Vermillion River by Louis Vieux, a Potawatomi Indian chief. He sells and trades goods with emigrants.

Fort Kearny is established, named in honor of Stephen Watts Kearny.

Thomas "Peg Leg" Smith establishes a trading post along the Bear River. This is near where Idaho, Utah, and Wyoming meet today.

Carson Pass is named in honor of Kit Carson.

The town of Sacramento is founded on Johann Sutter's land.

African-American mountain man James Beckwourth serves as a scout for Frémont.

1849

Estimated traffic on trails in 1849: 30,000. (The reason for the sudden huge increase: *gold.*)

Spring   The California Gold Rush begins.

June 9–11   The region around Ash Hollow and Chimney Rock is battered by severe thunderstorms, torrential rain, and hail. Horses and oxen are struck by lightning.

July 19   The Hudspeth Cutoff is established by Benoni M. Hudspeth.

November 13   Californians draft a constitution and formally request statehood.

Other Events of 1849

Ferry service across the Missouri River starts at St. Joseph.

Fort John's name is officially changed to Fort Laramie (it had been informally called that for years). It also becomes a U.S. military post, after having been run by traders.

This is a good, rainy (but not excessively rainy) year on the plains, providing lots of grass for draft animals. But because of the wet conditions, cholera is common on the trails. Epidemics break out along the Red Vermillion River, the Platte River, and the North Platte River as far west as Fort Laramie.

Fort Vancouver becomes a full-fledged U.S. military post.

A stagecoach line opens between Independence, Missouri, and Santa Fe.

Mormon Station is established in Nevada's Carson Valley. (The Mormons consider Nevada to be part of their "State of Deseret.")

1850

Estimated traffic on trails in 1850: 55,000. (More people and wagons travel the trails this year than any other.)

May   **The U.S. army stockade at The Dalles expands to a full-fledged army post called Camp Drum.**

July 1   Monthly mail coaches and stagecoaches begin to travel the trail between Independence and Great Salt Lake City.

September 9   California becomes a state. New Mexico and Utah are formally organized as territories.

September 27   The Donation Land Act provides free land for settlers in the Oregon Territory. (Before this, land was mostly up for grabs, with little or no rhyme or reason.) Now any male citizen who settles in the Oregon Territory can claim, free of charge, up to 320 acres, plus an additional 320 acres in his wife's name. Settlers must live on their claim for at least four years, or they lose title. Nor can they sell the land until the four years are up.

Other Events of 1850

Smith's Trading Post is abandoned.

The "Cayuse War" ends.

A steam ferry operates at St. Joseph, speeding up the time it takes to cross the Missouri River.

James Beckwourth discovers a pass (which becomes known as Beckwourth Pass) through the Sierra Nevadas near present-day Reno. He soon establishes an alternate route into California, known as the Beckwourth Route.

This spring and summer are unusually dry, resulting in a shortage of grass on the plains. Meanwhile, the cholera epidemic gets worse.

The "Mariposa War" erupts in California between settlers and the Miwok and Yokut Indians.

1851

Estimated traffic on trails in 1851: 10,000.

July 23   Signing of the Treaty of Traverse des Sioux between the Lakota Indians and the U.S. government. The Lakota give up nearly all their land in Iowa.

Other Events of 1851

Negotiations for the Fort Laramie Treaty take place. Plains Indians (about 10,000) assemble at Horse Creek, 35 miles southeast of Fort Laramie.

The capital of Oregon Territory is moved from Oregon City to Salem, farther up the Willamette Valley.

1852

Estimated traffic on trails in 1852: 50,000.

Trouble breaks out between settlers and Modoc Indians near Tule Lake in northern California and southern Oregon. Many deaths and outrages occur on both sides. Sporadic fighting continues until September 1853, when a negotiated settlement is reached.

Ulysses S. Grant is briefly stationed with the U.S. Infantry at Fort Vancouver. He's reassigned to California the following year.

Ezra Meeker is a member of a wagon train that arrives in Oregon. More than a half-century later, in 1906, he'll return east, retracing the Oregon Trail by memory. In the process he performs a valuable service for historians and tourists alike.

A cholera epidemic sweeps the area between Fort Kearny and Ash Hollow.

A free bridge is built across the North Platte River, replacing the Mormon ferry.

1853

Estimated traffic on trails in 1853: 20,000.

March 2   Washington Territory is separated from Oregon Territory.

September   A negotiated settlement temporarily ends hostilities between settlers and the Modocs in northern California and southern Oregon.

Other Events of 1853

A toll bridge is built across Thomas Fork.

Camp Drum is renamed Camp Dalles.

A steam ferry operates at Kanesville, Iowa, for crossing the Missouri River.

The Donation Land Act of 1850 is amended. Settlers can buy unclaimed land for $1.25 per acre if they live on it for at least two years.

1854

Estimated traffic on trails in 1854: 10,000.

May 26   Kansas and Nebraska are divided into two separate territories (by the Kansas-Nebraska Act) with "popular sovereignty" regarding slavery.

July   Vast tracts of eastern Kansas and Nebraska are opened to homesteading.

August   A Mormon party traveling along the North Platte River claims that a cow has been stolen by Lakota Indians, which leads to hostilities a few days later.

August 19   The peace of the Fort Laramie Treaty is broken by Lt. John L. Grattan, resulting in the "Grattan Massacre" nine miles southeast of Fort Laramie. Lt. Grattan and all but one of his men, as well as Lakota chief Conquering Bear, are killed. Subsequent Indian attacks occur along that stretch of the trail.

August 20   The "Ward Massacre": A wagon train led by Alexander Ward is attacked by Indians 20 miles east of Fort Boise, killing all but two of its 40 emigrants. Retaliations follow, and it's tense and dangerous along this stretch of trail for the rest of the decade, with frequent attacks on small parties.

Other Events of 1854

The town of Omaha, Nebraska, is founded near Winter Quarters, but most trail traffic bypasses it.

Due to hostilities following the "Ward Massacre," Fort Boise is abandoned.

The Kansas towns of Lawrence and Topeka are founded.

Frederick W. Lander opens a trading post and begins to survey and clear the Lander Cutoff (which won't be completed until 1858).

Sacramento becomes the capital of California.

1855

Estimated traffic on trails in 1855: 5,000.

January 16   Omaha is designated the capital of the Nebraska Territory.

May   At the Walla Walla Council in Walla Walla Valley, Governor Isaac Stevens persuades some—but not all—leaders of the Nez Perce, Cayuse, Umatilla, Walla Walla, and Yakima Indians to surrender large tracts of land in exchange for various guarantees and promises. This agreement is violated by the government and settlers less than two weeks later. The "Yakima War" begins between settlers and local Indian nations.

August   Two competing pro- and anti-slavery legislatures claim legitimacy in Kansas.

September 3   Gen. William S. Harney leads troops from Fort Kearny in an attack on the Lakota village of Chief Little Thunder near Ash Hollow. This is known as the "Battle of Blue Water."

October   A virtual civil war erupts in eastern Kansas between pro- and anti-slavery settlers. Kansas begins to be known as "Bleeding Kansas."

Other Events of 1855

Robidoux Pass Trading Post is abandoned, largely because Oregon Trail traffic has been re-routed through the newly opened Mitchell Pass, avoiding Robidoux Pass altogether.

Abolitionist John Brown settles with his sons in Kansas and becomes a leader among the anti-slavery guerrillas there.

Political and sometimes armed disputes break out in Kansas over slavery.

Lewis Robinson, a Mormon, purchases Fort Bridger from Jim Bridger.

1856

Estimated traffic on trails in 1856: 5,000.

March 26	Klickitat and Yakima Indians attack The Dalles, burning part of the town and killing settlers.
May 21	Pro-slavery forces attack Lawrence, Kansas, killing one man.
May 24	Retaliating for the attack on Lawrence, John Brown's anti-slavery group attacks the pro-slavery settlement at Pottawatomie Creek, where five men are dragged from their homes and killed.
July 4	Federal troops disperse the officially illegal free-soil legislature at Topeka, Kansas.
July 20	The great "Handcart Migration" of Mormons from Florence, Nebraska, to Great Salt Lake City begins.
September 15	Federal troops prevent an army of pro-slavery Missourians, known as "border ruffians," from invading Kansas.
Early November	**A terrible autumn blizzard maroons emigrants near Willow Springs, Independence Rock, and Devil's Gate, leading to more than 100 deaths.**

Other Events of 1856

Winter Quarters, Nebraska, is renamed Florence. By now few Mormons live here, but the town is a frequent stop for both Mormon and non-Mormon emigrants.

Indians in southern Oregon fight against settlers in the "Rogue River Indian Wars."

1857

Estimated traffic on trails in 1857: 5,000.

January 15   A pro-slavery legislature convenes in Lecompton, Kansas.

September 11   The "Mormon War" begins. Mormon fanatic John D. Lee, angry over U.S. President Buchanan's order that Brigham Young step down as governor of Utah, incites other Mormons and a band of Indians to murder a group of 120 emigrants bound for California at Mountain Meadow, Utah.

Other Events of 1857

The Hollenberg Ranch waystation is founded.

Mormons abandon and burn Fort Bridger.

1858

Estimated traffic on trails in 1858: 10,000.

October 9   The Overland Mail stagecoach completes its first trip from San Francisco to Missouri in 23 days. Another stagecoach going in the opposite direction completes the trip two days later.

Other Events of 1858

Fort Bridger is rebuilt as a U.S. military installation.

Rock Creek Station is founded.

Lander Cutoff opens.

C. C. Mills, a member of an Army engineer party, becomes the first photographer to travel the Oregon Trail, taking pictures of emigrants and landmarks.

Ferry service begins at the McDonald Ford of the John Day River.

The "Mormon War" ends.

Carson City is founded, named after Kit Carson.

1859

Estimated traffic on trails in 1859: 30,000.

February 14   Oregon becomes a state.

June   The Comstock Lode silver mine is discovered on Henry Comstock's land in Nevada. A silver rush begins.

Other Events of 1859

The "Yakima War" ends.

Thirty-two Mile Station and Midway Station are established.

Farmers settle in the vicinity of Rock Creek Station and Big Sandy.

A free bridge is built across the Blue River near Independence.

A provisional government for Nevada Territory is created, with Isaac Roop serving as provisional governor.

Virginia City is founded near the Comstock Lode.

1860

Estimated traffic on trails in 1860: 15,000.

April 3   Pony Express mail service begins. Riders can carry mail from St. Joseph, Missouri, to Sacramento, California, in about eight days. Thirty-two Mile Station, Midway Station, and Fort Kearny, among others, become Pony Express stations. Stations are also established at Split Rock, Three Crossings, Ice Spring Slough, Lander Cutoff, Pacific Springs, and other locations along the western trails.

September 9   During the "Otter Massacre" east of Givens Hot Springs, Indians lay siege to circled wagons for three days. Only 12 out of 44 emigrants survive.

Other Events of 1860

British writer and adventurer Richard Burton travels the Oregon Trail by stagecoach to Great Salt Lake City. He later publishes an account of his trip.

Samuel L. Clemens (later known as Mark Twain) travels the Oregon and California Trails. He settles briefly in western Nevada, near the site of the Comstock Lode silver strikes.

The "Paiute War" in the Carson and Truckee Valleys of Nevada erupts after two Indian girls are abducted by white traders.

Fort Churchill is established in Nevada as a result of the "Paiute War."

PRONUNCIATION GUIDE

How do you say Nauvoo? Below are some pronunciations for those odd sounding names in *Oregon Trail II.*

anise	ANN-is
Ayers Natural Bridge	AIRS
Barlow Toll Road	BAR-low
Bonneville Point	BON-nee-vill
Bruneau	broo-NO (like the name "Bruno" but with the accent on the second syllable)
butte (as in Church Butte)	BYOOT (sounded like the first syllable of the word "beautiful")
cholera	CALL-er-uh

The Dalles	DALS (rhymes with "gals" and "pals")
Deschutes	duh-SHOOTS
Fort Boise	BOY-zee
Fort Kearny	CAR-nee
Genoa	juh-NO-uh (it's named for the famous Italian city, but pronounced differently)
Grande Ronde	GRAND ROND
the grippe	GRIP
Guittard's Station	gee-TARDS (similar to the word "guitar")
Hudspeth Cutoff	HUDS-peth
Ice Spring Slough	SLEW
Jameson's Station	JAME-uh-sons (the first syllable rhymes with "game")
Kennekuk Station	KEN-uh-kuck
Klamath	CLAM-uth
laudanum	LAW-duh-num
lecithin	LESS-uh-thin
Loup River	LOOP
Malad River	muh-LAD
Malheur River	mal-HYUR (the last syllable sounds like the first syllable of "Huron")
Mount Pisgah Waystation	PIZZ-gah
Nauvoo	NAW-voo
Oregon	despite the fact that many people pronounce it or-uh-GON, the generally preferred pronunciation of Oregon (particularly preferred by the Oregonians themselves) is OR-uh-gun, with the accent on the first syllable

Pahute Peak	PAH-yoot
pemmican	PEM-uh-can (almost rhymes with "pelican")
Pequop Mountains	PEE-kwop
Placerville	PLAS-er-vill (the first syllable rhymes with "glass")
Platte River	PLAT (rhymes with "hat")
Robidoux Pass	ROE-buh-DOE
saleratus	SAL-er-AY-tus
Siskiyou Mountains	SIS-key-YOU
Sublette Cutoff	SUB-lit
Toano Range	TOE-uh-NO (some other "Toanos" in the United States, however, are pronounced toe-AN-oh)
Tooele Valley	too-EL-uh
Truckee	TRUCK-ee
Tygh Valley	TIE
Umatilla River	YOU-muh-TILL-uh
Vermillion River	ver-MILL-yun (rhymes with "per million")
Weber River	WEE-ber (believe it or not, that's how the river's name is pronounced!)
Willamette Valley	will-LAM-it

THE PEOPLE BEHIND OREGON TRAIL II

The Oregon Trail II *core design team (l-r): Steve Splinter, Wayne Studer, Charolyn Kapplinger, and Craig Copley.*

Not counting the more than 20-year history of *The Oregon Trail*, nearly two full years of new research, design, and production have gone into making *Oregon Trail II*. And over a hundred people have been involved in this creation.

The core design team has worked on the program from the beginning, and consists of four longtime MECC staff members whose expertise adds up to over 50 years of educational computing. That's not even counting all the other people who worked on the program!

The four members of the core design team are:

Producer Craig Copley. Few people have worked at MECC longer or been involved in more projects here than Copley. He joined the company in 1976, just three years after its founding. Starting out as a programmer, today he is MECC's Director of New Media. He produces projects that include *The Oregon Trail, The Amazon Trail,* and *The Yukon Trail,* along with the *GeoGraph* series (*World GeoGraph, USA GeoGraph,* and *Canada GeoGraph.*)

Project Director/Historian/Writer Wayne Studer. Studer has been with MECC since 1983. As a software designer, he's developed a number of programs including the entire *GeoGraph* series, the MECC *Dataquest* series, the *Time Navigator* series, *Super Munchers,* and every version of *The Oregon Trail* published since 1990. (This includes its cooperative-learning spin-off, *Wagon Train 1848.*)

Studer holds B.A. and M.A. degrees in English from the College of William and Mary, and a Ph.D. in American Studies from the University of Minnesota, specializing in nineteenth-century U.S. history and culture. (That certainly came in handy!) He's also taught American Studies, writing, and communications.

Lead Programmer Steven D. Splinter. While attending the University of Minnesota's Institute of Technology in 1984, Splinter worked at MECC as a part-time student programmer. Two years later he became a full-time staff member. He's worked on a great many MECC programs on the Apple II, IIGS, BBC Acorn, Macintosh, MS-DOS, and Windows platforms.

Among Splinter's more recent projects as Lead Programmer and co-designer are the entire *GeoGraph* series, *Super Munchers, Odell Down Under,* and four different versions of *The Oregon Trail* before *Oregon Trail II.*

Lead Artist Charolyn Kapplinger. Since coming to MECC in 1984, Kapplinger has created on-screen art for more than 200 Apple II, Apple IIGS, MS-DOS, Windows, and Macintosh programs. Among them are the *Storybook Weaver* series, the *Muncher* series, *World GeoGraph, USA GeoGraph, Zoyon Patrol, TesselMania!, Odell Lake, Wonderland Puzzles, The Amazon Trail,* and every version of *The Oregon Trail* published during the past 11 years. She holds a B.A. degree in Art and Elementary Education, and a Certificate in Programming and Operations from the Control Data Institute of Minneapolis.

Other programmers who worked extensively on *Oregon Trail II* are **Beth H. Daniels** (who made the Guidebook and Glossary work so nicely), **Susan M. Gabrys** (who worked on the underlying health model, among other things), **Kevin A. Job** (all sorts of things on the Windows side), **John Ojanen** (he got hunting to work), **James L. Thompson** (early hunting and "building blocks" work), and **Douglas N. Wheeler** (rafting and early Windows tasks). Additional programming was done by **Vincent J. Erickson**, **Lon Koenig**, **Al Lathrop**, **Tom Naughton**, **Alan B. Nelson**, **Brian S. Nesse**, **Randy E. Rasmussen**, **Kirk Sumner**, **Richard Wells**, and **Jeff White**.

Other artists who made major contributions to *Oregon Trail II* are **Tim Courteau** (who worked mostly on the human beings in the program), **John Diebel** (he's responsible for all of those lovely 3-D rendered towns, forts, and interiors), **Sandra Forslund** (landscapes for days!), **Jan Tockman** (she "winterized" everything in the program and added people to scenes), **Michael Tschimperle** (lots and lots of stuff, including people, animals, hunting scenes, and the animated opening title sequence), and **Dave Wood** (newspapers, wanted posters, text screens, and various concluding scenes).

Still other artwork was done by **Craig Copley**, **Dee Dee Daus**, **Dave Denninger**, **Steven D. Splinter**, **Wayne Studer**, and **Donna Maria Waltz**.

Photography and videography work was done by **Craig Copley**, **Dee Dee Daus**, **Sara Ann Garvey**, **Charolyn Kapplinger**, **John Ojanen**, **Tracy Schruth-Panning**, **Wayne Studer**, **Michael Tschimperle**, **Paul Wieser**, and **Dave Wood**.

Additional photographic images were obtained courtesy **Accent Media Productions, Inc.**

Besides his duties as artist, **Michael Tschimperle** also did makeup. And he took care of the costuming, too (with help from the **Theatrical Costume Company of Minneapolis**). Versatile guy.

Stock footage was obtained courtesy of the following agencies and institutions: **Accent Media Productions, Inc.**; **Archive Photos, Inc.**; **EMA Video Productions, Inc.**; **The University of St. Thomas**; and **The WPA Film Library**.

Video production work was performed by **Sara Ann Garvey**, **Michael Tschimperle** (him again!), **Paul Wieser**, and **Janet Wolnik**, with additional video courtesy **Accent Media Productions, Inc.**

The audio/video dialogue sequencing (a nifty little process also known as "phonemic synchronization") was handled by **Ruth Kivisto** and **Korey Schulz**.

Characters' dialogue was written by **Catherine Baxter** and **Wayne Studer**, who also wrote the "automatic" diary entries.

Larry Phenow was the music coordinator for *Oregon Trail II*. The original soundtrack was composed by **Eric Speier** for **Speier Productions, Inc.**

Additional music was written and/or performed by **Glen Anderson**, **William Pensoneau**, **Larry Phenow**, **Eric Speier**, and **Mark Stillman**.

Sound/audio production tasks were done by **Glen Anderson**, **Sara Ann Garvey**, **Chad Iverson**, **Lon Koenig**, **Larry Phenow**, and **Paul Wieser**. Sound effects were created or obtained by **Glen Anderson**, **Lon Koenig**, and **Larry Phenow**. (Funny how some of these names keep popping up over and over again.)

The American Indian culture consultants for the project were **Rich Bergeron**, **Levi Eagle Feather**, **Cherie Neima**, and **William Pensoneau**. Spanish translation was provided by **Claudio Valenzuela**, who also served as our Hispanic culture consultant.

The Lead Tester of *Oregon Trail II* was **Mark Schneider**, with additional testing done by **Brian Anderson**, **Rose Enriquez**, **Marty Euerle**, **Todd George**, **Jody Johnson**, **Mark Larson**, **Josef Ling**, **Barry Mansur**, **Timothy Roseth**, **Troy Small**, **Wayne Studer**, **Vang Thao**, and **Dawn Wichmann**.

Documentation was done by **Catherine Baxter** and **Wayne Studer**, with editing by **Ray Kush**. **Catherine Baxter** also produced the on-line help features of the simulation. This book was edited by **Zu Vincent** and designed and laid out by **Danielle Foster**. **Jennifer Fox** was the Project Editor.

Various packaging and promotional chores were taken care of by **Kathy Quinby**, **Brad Schrag**, and **Grace Trombetta**. Additional vital promotional tasks were performed by **Pat Kallio**, **Michelle LeMay**, and **Tracy Schruth-Panning**. Contract work, negotiations, and other legal matters (ah, what would we do without them?) were handled by **Todd Brown**, **Paul Gullickson**, **Diane Perry-Moore**, and **Paul Wieser**.

Management support was provided by **Craig Copley**, **Greg Holey**, **John Krenz**, **Sherry Olson**, **Diane Portner**, **Kathy Quinby**, **Steve Taffee**, and **Grace Trombetta**.

The text of the opening title sequence was written by **Wayne Studer** and narrated by **John Arthur Olson**.

Roughly a hundred people acted out the roles of the almost 200 characters in *Oregon Trail II*. Rather than list all of them here, we heartily recommend that you use the program's *About Oregon Trail II* feature (under the Apple menu on the Macintosh and under the Help menu on Windows) to see a detailed recapitulation of all the credits, including the actors. You won't regret it.

The title screen painting, by the way, is "Westward the Course of Empire Takes Its Way," painted in 1860 by **Emanuel Leutze**. This painting is used with permission from the **Smithsonian Institution**. Leutze is perhaps best known for his 1851 painting "Washington Crossing the Delaware." (Have you ever wondered whether Washington was actually standing up when he crossed the river in that little boat?)

The Guidebook "Advice" text is based on an 1849 publication (now in the public domain), *Accompaniment to the Map of the Emigrant Road from Independence, Mo., to San Francisco, California*, by **T.H. Jefferson**. **Wayne Studer** made edits, deletions, and additions to make it more helpful for users.

Except for historical individuals, the characters depicted in this software program are fictional and are not intended to represent or suggest any other specific persons. Any resemblance or similarity whatsoever to any other persons, fictional or nonfictional, living or dead, are entirely unintentional and coincidental.

Aren't you glad you asked?

SELECTED BIBLIOGRAPHY

More than 200 primary and secondary sources were consulted in the extensive research that went into creating *Oregon Trail II* and ensuring its historical and geographical accuracy. It would be impractical to try to list all of these sources here, but the following selected bibliography cites the books that consistently proved most useful and provided the greatest amount of information actually incorporated into the program. If you're interested in learning more about the western trails, you may be able to find many of these books at your local library.

Primary (First-hand) Sources

Barton, Lois, ed. *One Woman's West: Recollections of the Oregon Trail and Settling the Northwest Country by Martha Gay Masterson, 1838–1916.* Spencer Butte Press, 1986.

Brown, William Richard. *An Authentic Wagon Train Journal of 1853 from Indiana to California*. Barbara Wills, ed. Horseshoe Printing, 1985.

Clayton, William. *The Latter-Day Saints' Emigrants' Guide*. Stanley B. Kimball, ed. Reprint (originally published 1847). The Patrice Press, 1983.

Dawson, Charles. *Pioneer Tales of the Oregon Trail and of Jefferson County*. Crane & Company, 1912.

Gordon, Mary, ed. *Overland to California with the Pioneer Line: The Gold Rush Diary of Bernard J. Reid*. The Patrice Press, 1983.

Holmes, Kenneth L., ed. *Covered Wagon Women: Diaries and Letters from the Western Trails, 1840–1890. Volume 1: 1840–1849*. The Arthur H. Clark Company, 1983.

Jefferson, T.H. *Accompaniment to the Map of the Emigrant Road from Independence, Mo., to San Francisco, California*. 1849; no other publication data.

Marcy, Randolph B. *The Prairie Traveler: A Handbook for Overland Explorations*. Reprint (originally published 1859). Applewood Books, no date.

Meeker, Ezra. *Ox-Team Days on the Oregon Trail*. World Book Company, 1924.

Parde, Charles Ross. *Dreams to Dust: A Diary of the California Gold Rush, 1849–1850*. James E. Davis, ed. University of Nebraska Press, 1989.

Parkman, Francis. *The Oregon Trail*. Reprint (originally published 1849). The New American Library, 1950.

Preuss, Charles. *Topographical Map of the Road from Missouri to Oregon… in Seven Sections*. E. Weber and Company, 1846.

Webber, Bert, ed. *The Oregon and Applegate Trail Diary of Welborn Beeson in 1853*. Webb Research Group, 1987.

Webber, Bert, ed. *The Oregon and California Trail Diary of Jane Gould in 1862*. Webb Research Group, 1987.

Webber, Bert, ed. *The Oregon and Overland Trail Diary of Mary Louisa Black in 1865*. Webb Research Group, 1989.

Webber, Bert, ed. *The Oregon Trail Diary of James Akin, Jr., in 1852*. Webb Research Group, 1989.

Webber, Bert, ed. *The Oregon Trail Diary of Rev. Edward Evans Parrish in 1844*. Webb Research Group, 1988.

Webber, Bert, ed. *The Oregon Trail Diary of Twin Sisters, Cecelia Adams and Parthenia Blank in 1852*. Webb Research Group, 1992.

Secondary Sources

Dary, David. *Entrepreneurs of the Old West*. University of Nebraska Press, 1986.

DeVoto, Bernard. *Across the Wide Missouri*. Reprint. Houghton Mifflin Company, 1947.

Dodd, Lawrence. *Narcissa Whitman on the Oregon Trail*. Ye Galleon Press, 1985.

Dunlop, Richard. *Great Trails of the West*. Abington, 1971.

Fanselow, Julie. *The Traveler's Guide to the Oregon Trail*. Falcon Press, 1992.

Federal Writers' Project. *The Oregon Trail: The Missouri River to the Pacific Ocean*. Reprint (originally published 1939). Hastings House, 1972.

Fisher, Leonard E. *The Oregon Trail*. Holiday House, 1990.

Franzwa, Gregory M. *Maps of the Oregon Trail*. Third edition. The Patrice Press, 1990.

Franzwa, Gregory M. *The Oregon Trail Revisited*. Fourth edition. The Patrice Press, 1988.

Graydon, Charles K. *Trail of the First Wagons Over the Sierra Nevada*. The Patrice Press, 1986.

Haines, Aubrey L. *Historic Sites Along the Oregon Trail*. The Patrice Press, 1981.

Harris, E.W. *The Overland Emigrant Trail to California*. Nevada Emigrant Trail Marking Committee/ Nevada Historical Society, 1986.

Hill, William E. *The Oregon Trail, Yesterday and Today: A Brief History and Pictorial Journey Along the Wagon Tracks of Pioneers*. Caxton Printers, 1987.

Holliday, J.S. *The World Rushed In: The California Gold Rush Experience*. Simon and Schuster, 1981.

Horan, James D. *The Great American West: A Pictorial History from Coronado to the Last Frontier*. Bonanza Books, 1959.

Hunt, Thomas H. and Robert V.H. Adams. *Ghost Trails to California*. American West Publishing Company, 1974.

Kimball, Stanley B. *Historic Sites and Markers Along the Mormon and Other Great Western Trails*. University of Illinois Press, 1988.

Lavender, David. *The Overland Migrations: Settlers to Oregon, California, and Utah*. U.S. National Park Service, 1980.

Lavender, David. *Westward Vision: The Story of the Oregon Trail*. University of Nebraska Press, 1963.

Mattes, Merrill. *The Great Platte River Road*. Nebraska State Historical Society, 1969.

Moffit, Gwen. *Hard Road West: Alone on the California Trail*. Viking Press, 1981.

Murphy, Dan and Gary Ladd. *Oregon Trail: Voyage of Discovery—The Story Behind the Scenery*. KC Publications, Inc., 1992.

National Park Service. *Comprehensive Management and Use Plan: Oregon National Historic Trail—Selected Historic Sites and Cross-Country Segments*. U.S. Department of the Interior, 1981.

Nicholas, Jonathan and Ron Cronin. *On the Oregon Trail*. Graphic Arts Center Publishing Company, 1993.

The Oregon-California Trails Association.

Paden, Irene D. *Prairie Schooner Detours*. The Patrice Press, 1990.

Paden, Irene D. *The Wake of the Prairie Schooner*. McMillan and Company, 1947.

Richmond, Robert W. and Robert W. Mardock, eds. A *Nation Moving West: Readings in the History of the American Frontier*. University of Nebraska Press, 1966.

Rounds, Glen. *The Prairie Schooner*. Holiday House, Inc., 1968.

Rumer, Thomas A. *The Wagon Trains of '44: A Comparative View of the Individual Caravans in the Emigration of 1844 to Oregon*. A.H. Clark, 1989.

Schlesinger, Arthur M., Jr. *The Almanac of American History*. Perigree Books, 1983.

Shellenberger, Robert. *Wagons West: Trail Tales 1848.* Heritage West Books, 1991.

Stein, R. Conrad. *The Story of the Oregon Trail.* Childrens Press, 1984.

Stewart, George Rippey. *The California Trail.* McGraw Hill Book Company, 1962.

Unruh, John D., Jr. *The Plains Across: The Overland Emigrants and the Trans-Mississippi West, 1840–60.* University of Illinois Press, 1979.

VanSteenwyk, Elizabeth. *The California Gold Rush: West with the Forty-niners.* F. Watts, 1991.

Viola, Herman J. *Exploring the West.* Smithsonian Books, 1987.

Worcester, Don, ed. *Pioneer Trails West, by the Western Writers of America.* Caxton Printers, 1985.

Wright, Frank. *The Pioneering Adventure in Nevada.* Nevada Historical Society, no date.

Finally, if you're a really big fan of *Oregon Trail II* (and we certainly hope you are!) and want to learn more about the old western trails, consider joining the Oregon-California Trails Association (OCTA for short). The OCTA publishes a glossy quarterly magazine titled *Overland Journal* and a monthly newsletter called *News from the Plains,* both full of information about the trails. The OCTA also sponsors an annual convention. For more information, contact the OCTA at P.O. Box 1019, Independence, MO 64051-0519.

INDEX

Computer Game Books

1942: The Pacific Air War-The Official Strategy Guide	$19.95
The 7th Guest: The Official Strategy Guide	$19.95
Aces Over Europe: The Official Strategy Guide	$19.95
Aegis: Guardian of the Fleet-The Official Strategy Guide	$19.95
Alone in the Dark 3: The Official Strategy Guide	$19.95
Armored Fist: The Official Strategy Guide	$19.95
Betrayal at Krondor: The Official Strategy Guide	$19.95
Blackthorne: The Official Strategy Guide	$14.95
CD-ROM Games Secrets, Volume 1	$19.95
Cyberia: The Official Strategy Guide	$19.95
Computer Adventure Games Secrets	$19.95
Descent: The Official Strategy Guide	$19.95
Donkey Kong Country Game Secrets the Unauthorized Edition	$9.95
DOOM Battlebook	$14.95
DOOM II: The Official Strategy Guide	$19.95
Dracula Unleashed: The Official Strategy Guide & Novel	$19.95
Dragon Lore: The Official Strategy Guide	$19.95
Fleet Defender: The Official Strategy Guide	$19.95
Front Page Sports Baseball '94: The Official Playbook	$19.95
Front Page Sports Football Pro '95: The Official Playbook	$19.95
Harpoon II: The Official Strategy Guide	$19.95
Heretic: The Official Strategy Guide	$19.95
Kingdom: The Far Reaches-The Official Strategy Guide	$14.95
King's Quest VII: The Unauthorized Strategy Guide	$19.95
The Legend of Kyrandia: The Official Strategy Guide	$19.95
Lemmings: The Official Companion (with disk)	$24.95
Lode Runner: The Legend Returns-The Official Strategy Guide	$19.95
Machiavelli the Prince: Official Secrets & Solutions	$12.95
Marathon: The Official Strategy Guide	$19.95
Master of Orion: The Official Strategy Guide	$19.95
Master of Magic: The Official Strategy Guide	$19.95
Microsoft Arcade: The Official Strategy Guide	$12.95
Microsoft Flight Simulator: The Official Strategy Guide	$19.95
Microsoft Golf: The Official Strategy Guide	$19.95
Microsoft Space Simulator: The Official Strategy Guide	$19.95
Might and Magic Compendium: The Authorized Strategy Guide for Games I, II, III, and IV	$19.95
Myst: The Official Strategy Guide	$19.95
Outpost: The Official Strategy Guide	$19.95
Pagan: Ultima VIII-The Ultimate Strategy Guide	$19.95
The Pagemaster: Official CD-ROM Strategy Guide	$14.95
Panzer General: The Official Strategy Guide	$19.95
Perfect General II: The Official Strategy Guide	$19.95
Prince of Persia: The Official Strategy Guide	$19.95
Quest for Glory: The Authorized Strategy Guide	$19.95
Rebel Assault: The Official Insider's Guide	$19.95
Return to Zork Adventurer's Guide	$14.95
Shadow of the Comet: The Official Strategy Guide	$19.95
Sherlock Holmes, Consulting Detective: The Unauthorized Strategy Guide	$19.95
Sid Meier's Civilization, or Rome on 640K a Day	$19.95
Sid Meier's Colonization: The Official Strategy Guide	$19.95
SimCity 2000: Power, Politics, and Planning	$19.95
SimEarth: The Official Strategy Guide	$19.95
SimFarm Almanac: The Official Guide to SimFarm	$19.95
SimLife: The Official Strategy Guide	$19.95
SimTower: The Official Strategy Guide	$19.95
SSN-21 Seawolf: The Official Strategy Guide	$19.95
Star Crusader: The Official Strategy Guide	$19.95
Strike Commander: The Official Strategy Guide and Flight School	$19.95
Stunt Island: The Official Strategy Guide	$19.95
SubWar 2050: The Official Strategy Guide	$19.95
TIE Fighter: The Official Strategy Guide	$19.95
TIE Fighter: Defender of the Empire-Official Secrets & Solutions	$12.95
Ultima: The Avatar Adventures	$19.95
Ultima VII and Underworld: More Avatar Adventures	$19.95
Under a Killing Moon: The Official Strategy Guide	$19.95
WarCraft: Orcs & Humans Official Secrets & Solutions	$9.95
Wing Commander I, II, and III: The Ultimate Strategy Guide	$19.95
X-COM Terror From The Deep: The Official Strategy Guide	$19.95
X-COM UFO Defense: The Official Strategy Guide	$19.95
X-Wing: Collector's CD-ROM-The Official Strategy Guide	$19.95

Video Game Books

3DO Game Guide	$16.95
Behind the Scenes at Sega: The Making of a Video Game	$14.95
Boogerman Official Game Secrets	$12.95
Breath of Fire Authorized Game Secrets	$14.95
Complete Final Fantasy III Forbidden Game Secrets	$14.95
EA SPORTS Official Power Play Guide	$12.95
Earthworm Jim Official Game Secrets	$12.95
The Legend of Zelda: A Link to the Past-Game Secrets	$12.95
Lord of the Rings Official Game Secrets	$12.95
Maximum Carnage Official Game Secrets	$9.95
Mega Man X Official Game Secrets	$14.95
Mortal Kombat II Official Power Play Guide	$9.95
NBA JAM: The Official Power Play Guide	$12.95
GamePro Presents: Nintendo Games Secrets Greatest Tips	$11.95
Nintendo Games Secrets, Volumes 1, 2, 3, and 4	$11.95 each
Parent's Guide to Video Games	$12.95
Secret of Mana Official Game Secrets	$14.95
Sega CD Official Game Secrets	$12.95
GamePro Presents: Sega Genesis Games Secrets Greatest Tips, Second Edition	$12.95
Official Sega Genesis Power Tips Book, Volumes 2, and 3	$14.95 each
Sega Genesis Secrets, Volume 4	$12.95
Sega Genesis and Sega CD Secrets, Volume 5	$12.95
Sega Genesis Secrets, Volume 6	$12.95
Sonic 3 Official Play Guide	$12.95
Super Empire Strikes Back Official Game Secrets	$12.95
Super Mario World Game Secrets	$12.95
Super Metroid Unauthorized Game Secrets	$14.95
Super NES Games Secrets, Volumes 2, and 3	$11.95 each
Super NES Games Secrets, Volumes 4 and 5	$12.95 each
GamePro Presents: Super NES Games Secrets Greatest Tips	$11.95
Super NES Games Unauthorized Power Tips Guide, Volumes 1 and 2	$14.95 each
Super Star Wars Official Game Secrets	$12.95
TurboGrafx-16 and TurboExpress Secrets, Volume 1	$9.95
Urban Strike Official Power Play Guide, with Desert Strike & Jungle Strike	$12.95
Virtual Bart Official Game Secrets	$12.95

To Order Books

Please send me the following items:

Quantity #	Title	Unit Price	Total
_____	_____	$ _____	$ _____
_____	_____	$ _____	$ _____
_____	_____	$ _____	$ _____
_____	_____	$ _____	$ _____
_____	_____	$ _____	$ _____
_____	_____	$ _____	$ _____

Subtotal	$ _____
7.25% Sales Tax CA residents	$ _____
8.25% Sales Tax TN residents	$ _____
5.00% Sales Tax MD residents	$ _____
7.00% G.S.T. Canadian orders	$ _____
Shipping and Handling*	$ _____
Total Order	$ _____

*$4.00 shipping and handling charge for the first book and $1.00 for each additional book.

BY TELEPHONE: With Visa or MC, call (916) 632-4400 Mon.–Fri., 9–4 PST.
BY MAIL: Just fill out the information below and send with your remittance to:

Prima Publishing
P.O. Box 1260BK
Rocklin, CA 95677

Satisfaction unconditionally guaranteed

My name is _____

I live at _____

City _____ State _____ Zip _____

MC/Visa # _____ Exp. _____

Signature _____

Other Great Software Products from MECC!

MECC makes learning fun! If you like Oregon Trail II, try these other great new MECC CD-ROMs for both Windows and Macintosh computers!

Africa Trail™

Join an actual world record-setting bike expedition—Africa Trek—across modern-day Africa. Relive this adventure through the authentic photos and journal entries of the real-life team while learning about diverse people and places. Build critical thinking and problem-solving skills as you guide your team through the burning days and freezing nights of the Sahara and the lush rainforests of Zaire.

MayaQuest™—The Mystery Trail

A thousand years ago, one of the world's most advanced civilizations mysteriously collapsed. Join the MayaQuest bike team and travel across the Yucatan peninsula to explore why. Visit ancient archeological sites and, with a collection of high-tech tools, search for clues about this ancient culture. Authentic photographs from the actual 1995 expedition bring to life this great unsolved mystery.

And don't forget these other terrific CD-ROM products from MECC:

- The Amazon Trail®
- The Yukon Trail™
- Storybook Weaver® DELUXE
- Opening Night™
- Math Munchers™ DELUXE
- Troggle Trouble™ Math

Look for all these exciting titles at your favorite software retailer!